TIRPITZ
the floating fortress

TIRPITZ
the floating fortress

DAVID BROWN

NAVAL INSTITUTE PRESS

Published in the U.S.A. by the United States Naval Institute,
Annapolis, Maryland.
Library of Congress Catalog Card Number 76–062964.
© David Brown, 1977.
© Lionel Leventhal Limited, 1977.

Second impression 1978

Edited by Michael Boxall; designed by David Gibbons.
Printed by T. & A. Constable Limited, Edinburgh.

Contents

Introduction

The story of the last three days of the short life of the German battleship *Bismarck* is an epic of German courage and relentless British determination. The last battle, between *Bismarck* and the British battleships *Rodney* and *King George V*, set the seal on what was destined to become a legend after the German ship had sunk *Hood* and damaged *Prince of Wales* a few days earlier.

The facts were embellished by emotion—German pride in a battle against odds, British shame at the loss of *Hood*, an outdated, under-armoured and unmodernized ship which had been established as the epitome of British sea power by successive editors of *Jane's Fighting Ships* and the national press—and there emerged the myth of the virtually unsinkable battleship. It had taken a convulsive effort on the part of the Royal Navy to locate, track and destroy *Bismarck*, for no fewer than nine capital ships and three aircraft carriers had been given orders to take part in the hunt, convoys had been diverted and stripped of their heavy escorts—fortunately without consequent losses—and it was by no means certain that such an effort could ever be repeated.

That a repetition might be necessary was apparent to the Royal Navy, for it was known that *Bismarck*'s sister ship, *Tirpitz*, had begun sea trials in March 1941 —two months before the mid-Atlantic hunt. But *Tirpitz*, when she did move out from German waters, sailed not west but north, to lurk in Norwegian fiords as a threat to the heavily defended North Russian convoys. Her relatively long career was as inactive as *Bismarck*'s brief operational life had been hectic; her minor forays were unprofitable and her greatest single victory was attained without the need to close the enemy. For nearly three years she constrained the Royal Navy to retain two modern battleships in Northern waters, together with a valuable carrier which would almost invariably have been better employed elsewhere. British attempts to winkle *Tirpitz* out of her lair were as unsuccessful as all attacks on her up to September 1943. Thereafter, the 'floating battery' came under regular air attack until she was finally done to death in circumstances which reflected the lack of purpose and responsiveness only to be expected when a 'blue water' offensive instrument is finally relegated to a fixed defensive position in the Arctic shallows.

Technical note: throughout this volume, times are expressed according to naval usage. Thus, '1435' means 2.35pm.

1

Building a Battleship

Schlachtschiff 'G' was ordered early in 1936, was laid down in October of the same year and was launched with the name *Tirpitz* on 1 April 1937. Commissioned in December 1940, she was not, in fact, completed until February 1941.

No warship is built in a vacuum, springing fully-armed from the head of a constructor uninfluenced by international activities or national abilities. *Tirpitz* was a creation of her (German) times and one of 16 third-generation Dreadnought battleships conceived in the mid 1930s and completed between 1940 and 1942 in the shipyards of the United States, Japan, Italy, France and Britain, as well as Germany. The erstwhile members of the alliance which had contributed to the defeat of the Central Powers in 1918 had bound themselves to limit warship construction and had adhered to the terms of the Washington Naval Armaments Limitation Treaty from 1922 until 1930 (France and Italy) and the end of 1936 (Japan), observing in particular the moratorium on capital ship construction.

Germany had never been a party to the Washington Treaty, having been thoroughly limited by the 1919 Treaty of Versailles, which had left her with six pre-Dreadnought battleships, six light cruisers and two dozen destroyers and ocean-going torpedo-boats. Replacements for the battleships were not to exceed 10,000 tons (standard*) displacement, nor mount guns of greater calibre than 11in(280mm). The victors' capital ships were armed with guns of 12in(305mm) calibre and above, and the tonnage was the same as that agreed for heavy cruisers at Washington, insufficient to permit heavy armour protection and high speed and long range; the Allies had clearly envisaged some form of 'coast defence' monitor with no real deep water capability—they were less imaginative than the German naval planners.

Not until 1926 could the Weimar Republic see far

enough past its successive financial crises to permit planning for the replacement of the ancient battleships by a class of ships designed to remain within the Versailles limits. The naval staff officers and constructors responsible for evolving the design, excelled themselves and produced a ship which gave the other navies indigestible food for thought. By introducing powerful but economical diesel main propulsion machinery, using extensive welding in place of rivetting, and installing active stabilisers to compensate heavy topweight and a narrow beam, the new 'Panzerschiff' ('armoured ship') made nonsense of the 10,000-ton 8in(203mm) 'Treaty' cruisers, which were the largest gun-armed vessels allowed while the battleship moratorium was still in force. The 20,000-mile range, 26-knot 'pocket battleship' was armed with six 280mm (11in) guns in two turrets, eight single 150mm(5.9in) guns as secondary armament and eight 88mm(3.46in) anti-aircraft (AA) guns, and her machinery and magazines were armoured against 6in(152mm) shell fire and 500lb(227kg) bombs. Not surprisingly, the standard displacement was 1,700 tons in excess of that allowed by the Treaty of Versailles—an infraction which was not declared by the German Government when the first ship, *Deutschland*, was laid down in February 1929.

The signatories to the Washington Treaty had not intended that the German Navy should again emerge as an ocean-going power, and the appearance of this ship, which out-gunned nearly all the potential opponents that she could not out-run, stimulated protests which could not be legally sustained. Germany did, however, offer to cancel the construction of the ship, but the condition—admission as a full member of the Washington 'Club'—was politically unacceptable to France, although militarily it would have meant the continuation of the moratorium. At the conference which preceded the signature of the 1930 London Naval Treaty, her representatives gave notice of France's withdrawal from the clauses restricting the construction of capital ships and limiting the displace-

* Standard displacement was the weight of a ship fully stored and ammunitioned, lacking only oil fuel, lubricants and boiler feed water. This measurement was adopted as the yardstick of warship comparison and limitation—the 'standard' displacement.

ment of cruisers. Fascist Italy, claiming the right to parity of naval strength in the Mediterranean, followed France, and an arms race became inevitable.

The French answer to the *Deutschland* class, was a 26,500-ton 'fast battleship', armed with eight 330mm (13in) guns and possessing a sea speed of 29½ knots; radius of action—7,500nm—was appreciably less than that of the pocket battleship, but was quite adequate, bearing in mind France's geographical position and the availability of bases in all oceans. The first unit, *Dunkerque*, was approved in 1931, laid down at the end of 1932 (four months before the completion of *Deutschland*) and completed in April 1937. By the beginning of 1939, when *Strasbourg* joined her sister-ship in service, two more pocket battleships, *Admiral Scheer* and *Admiral Graf Spee* had long since been completed; furthermore, the German Navy had built two battlecruisers which were a direct challenge to the *Dunkerque* class.

The Weimar Republic, which had given Germany stability and democracy, gave way to the Nationalist Socialist Third Reich when Adolf Hitler became Chancellor in 1933. In October 1933, Hitler withdrew from the disarmament conferences and membership of the League of Nations, effectively repudiating the terms of the Treaty of Versailles. Thus freed, the German Navy had drawn up its plans for an answer to the new French ships, and had laid down two big battlecruisers, nominally of the same tonnage, in February 1934. *Scharnhorst* and *Gneisenau* were armed with *Deutschland*-type main armament turrets, originally ordered for three follow-on pocket battleships which were never laid down; they were thus somewhat under-armed by comparison with the *Dunkerque* class or the older British battlecruisers, but design work had already commenced on a 15in(380mm) twin turret which, in due course, would replace the 11in(280mm) triple turrets.

Considerable efforts have been made to define the exact type which the two German ships represented. For mainly prestige reasons, *Scharnhorst* and *Gneisenau* were designated 'Schlachtschiffe' ('battleships') rather than 'Panzerkreuzer' ('armoured cruisers'), which had been the First World War designation of the German equivalents to the British battlecruisers. In at least one respect, they were the equivalent of true line-of-battle ships, for their armour protection was heavy, with a total of 6.9in(175mm) in two armoured decks and 13in(330mm) at the waterline abreast the machinery and magazines; only two European battleships in service in 1939, the British *Nelson* and *Rodney*, had thicker armour. But from most aspects—comparable displacement, armament and propulsive power above

all—the German ship were battlecruisers (and would have been battlecruisers even when armed with six 380mm(15in) guns) able to run away from all but one of the capital ships armed with 15in or 16in (406mm) —*Hood*.

The Italian Navy was slower off the mark in designing, ordering and building its response to *Dunkerque*, but the *Littorio* class represented a considerable escalation in terms of size, gun calibre and, fortunately, building time compared with the other post-Treaty designs. *Littorio* and *Vittorio Veneto* had displacements exceeding 41,000 tons (although the Italians declared that they were adhering to the Treaty maximum of 35,000 tons) and were armed with nine 380mm(15in) guns in triple turrets. The scale of protection was the greatest yet, with 13.8in(350mm) on the waterline, and a total of 8.1in(207mm) horizontal protection over the vitals, while a new type of 'semi-external' anti-torpedo bulge ought to have been superior to underwater defence systems in foreign contemporary ships. The speed of the new Italian battleships was equally impressive, for they achieved more than 31 knots on trials and could sustain 28 knots sea speed; a large radius of action was not necessary, because the Italian Navy had no ocean-wide ambitions, only wild hopes of glory in the Mediterranean and Red Sea. Laid down in October 1934, the first two *Littorio*s were not ready for service until August 1940, three years after they had been launched. The delays were attributable to the country's lack of productive capacity for armour plate and large-calibre naval ordnance, and shortage of skilled technical manpower in the shipyards; both deficiencies were aggravated by the simultaneous modernization of four older battleships and the laying down in 1938 of two more *Littorio*-class ships, *Impero* and *Roma*.

For obvious reasons, France could not let Italy steal such a large march, and in 1935, two 'improved *Dunkerque* class' ships were ordered. These ships followed the same outline as the two earlier units, with the main armament concentrated in two quadruple turrets forward of the bridge, but they were larger and more powerful in every respect, with a standard displacement of 38,500 tons (again declared at 35,000 tons), a speed of more than 31 knots and an armament of eight 380mm(15in) guns. Armour protection was superior to that of the *Littorio* class and was, indeed, the thickest applied to any of the Western capital ships designed during the 1930s. *Richelieu*, the first unit of the new class, was laid down in October 1935 and completed in June 1940, when she escaped from France to Dakar; her sister-ship, *Jean Bart*, was not laid down until January 1939, but was launched in March 1940 and managed to get away to Casablanca, lacking all armament apart from some hastily installed light AA guns.

It was not in the nature of National Socialism to allow Germany to fall behind other European powers, but before embarking on the next stage of her naval building programme, the German Government concluded a treaty with Britain, ostensibly to limit the extent of the former's expansion. In fact, the Anglo-German Naval Agreement implied acceptance of Hitler's unilateral abrogation of the disarmament clauses in the Treaty of Versailles, three months earlier in March 1935, and bestowed legalized respectability on German naval re-armament. By allowing the German Navy to build up to 35 per cent of the Royal Navy's surface ship tonnage, the British Government thought to place a check on that re-armament; little attention appears to have been paid to the implication of an increase in the ocean-going strength of the German Navy, which could only be used aggressively and not in defence of a huge merchant marine essential to the survival of the nation. The signatories to the 1930 London Treaty could not lay down any capital ships before the end of 1936 at the earliest—the British Government had given the nod to Germany to permit battleship building up to a total of 183,750 tons (of which 82,000 tons had already gone on the pocket battleships and the two battlecruisers) at any time after 18 June 1935.

Initial studies into the design of a battleship had been in progress since 1932, and the design work on a 380mm(15in) twin turret had begun in 1934. Having accepted the London Treaty limit of 35,000 tons for individual battleships, the Germans decided to build two ships of this nominal displacement and, thanks to the efforts of the designers during the last six months of 1935, the contracts were placed in January 1936 for Battleships 'F' and 'G', soon to achieve fame as *Bismarck* and *Tirpitz*. The former was laid down on 1 June 1936, and the latter, on 24 October.

The Royal Navy ordered two 35,000-ton battleships in 1936, and laid the keels on 1 January 1937—both were to encounter *Bismarck* during the German ship's only operation. The US Navy, more concerned with staying ahead of the Imperial Japanese Navy, did not order its first new ships until 1937, but laid down the first, *North Carolina*, on 27 October of that year, nine days before the Japanese laid the keel of *Yamato*. The British opted for a ten-gun 14in(356mm) main armament, the US Navy for a nine-gun 16in(406mm) layout on 35,000 tons displacement, but the Japanese exceeded all previous limits by building a 63,000-ton behemoth which was armed with nine 460mm(18.1in) guns. All four of these ships were completed between December 1940 and December 1941, as well as a third unit of the British *King George V* class, all five of which had been laid down by mid 1937. Thus, ten modern battleships were completed during the 18 months up to December 1941, three in Britain, one in France, one in the United States, two in Italy, one in Japan and two in Germany.

The Design

German pre-1914 battleship design had proved extremely successful, for although there had been only two capital ship engagements of note during the First World War, at the Dogger Bank and Jutland, experience at the latter had shown that the German dreadnoughts were capable of withstanding British shellfire and that their guns were reliable and the fire-control systems accurate. The last two ships to be completed before the end of that war were *Baden* and *Bayern*, armed with 380mm(15in) guns and regarded as the German answer to the British *Queen Elizabeth* class. Taken to Scapa Flow after the German surrender, these ships had been closely inspected by Royal Navy Constructor Officers who had been much impressed with the protective arrangements, not only the armour, but also the internal sub-division and damage-control pumping system, and many German practices were subsequently adopted as standard for British warships.

The German designers of the inter-war period naturally turned to the last successful design of their predecessors when the time came to draw up the plans of a new class, and many features of the *Baden* class were perpetuated, although the new ships were to be capable of world-wide operations, whereas the old had been intended primarily for the North Sea.

One of the most significant changes was the 260 per cent increase in propulsive power to meet the demand for a 7½-knots increase in maximum speed—*Baden* had needed only 52,800shp to reach 22½ knots, *Bismarck* and *Tirpitz* reached 30 knots on 138,000shp. Large machinery spaces were provided, particularly to accommodate the twelve boilers in six separate compartments, thereby avoiding one of *Baden*'s main shortcomings—that of cramped engine and boiler rooms which had made repair and routine maintenance more difficult than was desirable. The ship's beam increased by 19ft(5.8m) to 118ft(35.97m), and in order to improve the 'fineness' so as to attain the specified maximum speed, the waterline length was increased by 168ft(51.2m) to 792ft(241.4m).

The inordinate beam, 10ft(3m) greater than that of any class apart from *Yamato*, has usually been explained by reference to the depth of the Kiel Canal and the approaches to the major German ports, with the corollary that large ships required a wide beam to reduce the draught. But *Tirpitz* at full load (53,500 tons) drew nearly 36ft(10.9m)—a foot more than the lighter but narrower (12½%) *King George V*. The wide beam was, in fact, adopted for reasons of stability; the width conferred high initial lateral stability, the resistance to roll making the ship a steady gunnery platform in heavy seas or an ocean swell. An important advantage could have been taken of the extra internal space, by incorporating wider 'internal bulges' for increased protection against underwater weapons such as torpedoes and contact mines. The depth of the watertight compartments between the boiler-room bulkhead and the ship's side in *Tirpitz* was some 16ft 9in(5.1m), so that the voids and liquid-filled spaces which were intended to absorb most of the energy loosed by an explosion, took up 28 per cent of the beam of the ship; by contrast, *King George V*'s 'sandwich' (void/liquid/void) was only 14ft 9in(4.5m) deep outboard of the boiler rooms, and took up 28.5 per cent of

the beam, in spite of having to 'shoe-horn' machinery for four shafts into a 103ft(31.4m)-wide hull. *Tirpitz* had only three shafts, and the two boiler rooms and one engine room ahead of each shaft were very large spaces offering improved steaming and maintenance conditions for the engineers, but each would have contained hundreds of tons of water had serious flooding occurred. In the case of the wing boiler rooms, if such flooding were to occur quickly on one side, the stability would be gravely imperilled by the increase of weight so far from the ship's centre-line.

The lengthening of the hull to compensate the beam brought further disadvantages, one of the most obvious being the increase in displacement, much of the extra structural weight being given over to the deck and waterline belt armour which had to protect all between the widely-separated fore- and aftermost 380mm(15in) turrets. The French reduced this distance to about 470ft (143m) in *Richelieu*, by concentrating all eight of the

Comparison of the principal characteristics of 'Tirpitz' and her contemporaries.

Class	Tirpitz	KGV	Richelieu	Littorio	N. Carolina
Nationality	German	British	French	Italian	American
Programme Year	1935	1936	1935	1934	1936
Laid Down	10 36	1 37	10 35	10 35	10 37
Launched	1 39	2 39	1 39	8 37	6 40
Completed	2 41	10 40	7 40	8 40	8 41
Dimensions:					
Length Overall	822ft(250.5m)	745ft(227m)	814ft(248m)	777ft(236.8m)	729ft(222m)
Beam	118ft(36m)	103ft(31.4m)	107⅔ft(32.8m)	108ft(32.9m)	108ft(32.9m)
Deep Draught	36ft(11m)	34½ft(10.5m)	35ft(10.7m)	34½(10.5m)	35ft(10.7m)
Displacement (tons):					
Standard	41,700	36,700	38,500	37,205	38,560
Full Load (1944)	53,500	44,460	47,161	45,963	46,770
Machinery:					
Shaft horse-power	163,000	114,000	179,000	139,561	121,000
Shafts	3	4	4	4	4
Sea Speed at Full Load in knots (designed)	30	28.25	30	30	27
Maximum speed at any load condition	31.1	29.25	32.5	31.3	26.8
Oil Fuel stowage (tons)	6,350	4,110	6,200	4,450	7,554
Armament (1944):*					
Surface Action	8x15in	10x14in	8x15in	9x15in	9x16in
	12x5.9in	—	—	12x6in	—
Dual Purpose	—	16x5.25in	9x6in	—	20x5in
Anti-Aircraft	16x4.1in	—	12x3.9in	12x3.5in	—
Close-Range	16x37mm	8x40mm	56x40mm	20x37mm	60x40mm
		64x2pdr			
	80x20mm	38x20mm	50x20mm	36x20mm	83x20mm
Aircraft	4	2	2	3	3
	Arado	Walrus	Loire 130	Ro 43	OS2U-1 3
	Ar 196A				
Protection (hull only):					
Main Belt (max)	12.6in(32cm)	15in(38cm)	15.75in(39cm)	13.8in(35cm)	12in(30cm)
Deck Total (max)	5.9in(15cm)	7in(18cm)	8.25in(21cm)	8.15in(20cm)	5in(13cm)
Complement (approx, 1944)	1,905	1,628	1,785	1,830	1,980

* *Littorio* '1944' data is actually the 1943 state.

380mm guns in two turrets ahead of the bridge, and saving some 3,000 tons in total armour weight compared with *Tirpitz*, which had a magazine-machinery-magazine length of nearly 560ft(170m). The other nations used a three-turret layout for nine or ten guns so that their 'vital spaces' were correspondingly shorter than those in *Tirpitz*.

The relationship of beam to length at the waterline has considerable bearing on the power required to attain a given maximum speed. The design figures for *Bismarck* and *Tirpitz* were 138,000shp to attain 30 knots with a length:beam ratio of 6.7:1; corresponding figures for contemporary classes were:

	L:B ratio	shp	max speed
King George V	7.1:1	110,000	28 knots
North Carolina	6.5:1	121,000	28 knots
Richelieu	7.4:1	150,000	30 knots
Littorio	7.0:1	130,000	30 knots
Yamato	6.9:1	150,000	27 knots

In the cases of the first four ships, whose actual trials displacements were similar, the designed power and speeds were considerably exceeded (in *Richelieu*, by 29,000shp and 2½ knots), with the exception of the British ship, which was hard pressed to make her designed speed, even with excess power. On trials, *Tirpitz* actually needed 163,000shp to reach her maximum speed of 31.1 knots, thanks to her relatively 'blunt' shape. The real penalty took the form of high fuel consumption at high cruising speeds, for more power was needed to force the ship along than was needed by a less portly hull: at 16 knots, *Tirpitz* steamed 1.13 miles for every ton of oil fuel burned—*King George V* covered 1.77 miles per ton at the same speed, while the relatively slender *Richelieu* was reputed to be able to attain 1.15 miles per ton at 20 knots. *Tirpitz* outranged the British and French battleships, but only because she carried 4,500 tons more fuel than *King George V* and 2,200 tons more than *Richelieu*.

Comparative data for 'Scharnhorst', 'Dunkerque' and 'Renown' after modernization.

	Scharnhorst	Dunkerque	Renown
Displacement (tons):			
Standard	31,800	26,500	32,000
Full load	—	c.31,000	36,080
Dimensions:			
Length Overall	741.5ft(226m)	702ft(214m)	794.25ft(242m)
Maximum Beam	98.5ft(30m)	101.7ft(31m)	101ft(30.8m)
Standard Draught	24.5ft(7.5m)	28ft(8.6m)	26.5ft(8m)
Machinery:	Geared Turbines in all three ships		
Shafts	3	4	4
Shaft Horse-Power	160,000	136,900	120,560
Trials Speed (knots)	31.5	31.1	30.1
Range (n. miles at knots)	10,000 at 19	—	7,500 at 15
Armanent:	3x3 11in	2x4 13in	3x2 15in
	6x2 5.9in	3x4 5.1in	10x2 4.5in AA
		+2x2 AA	
	7x2 4.1in AA	—	—
	8x2 37mm AAA	4x2 37mm AAA	3x8 2-pdr (40mm)
	10 20mm AAA	32 12.7mm AAA	16 0.5in AAA
Aircraft	4	2	3
Torpedo Tubes	2x3 21in (533mm)	None	8 21in (533mm)
Armour and Protective Plate:			
Deck Total	6.9in(175mm)	6.5in(165mm)	4in(102mm)
Waterline Belt	13in(330mm)	8.9in(225mm)	9in(228mm)
Weight of Plate (tons)	12,320	—	10,800
Complement	1,800	1,431	1,200

The German Navy was unique in designing and building three-shaft capital ships, a layout which they had adhered to for all their battleships (but not battlecruisers). It was continued in *Bismarck* and *Tirpitz* because it had proved to be successful and also because it was lighter than a four-shaft machinery installation of similar output—indeed, it was only 100 tons heavier than *King George V*'s considerably less powerful machinery. Under normal conditions, fully serviceable and undamaged, the three propellers and two rudders were sufficient for a good range of manoeuvrability, but a single torpedo hit on *Bismarck* broke a propeller shaft and jammed the rudders: insufficient turning moment could be applied by the undamaged wing shaft to counter the unwanted 15° of helm, and the battleship was rendered unmanoeuvrable in mid-ocean within reach of powerful enemies. It is probable that a four-shaft ship would have remained controllable after one such hit, and so the layout of *Bismarck*'s propulsive machinery was a major factor in her eventual loss.

The hull was more than 90 per cent welded, the major rivetted area being the side armour. A myth grew up concerning the nature of the armour used in the belt, the story-line being that it was made of a revolutionary new steel with a higher resistance to penetration than that used in other nations' armour. There was no basis of fact in this tale, which only served to build up the mystique surrounding the ships, for the Krupps 'Wotan' plate was simply another nickel-chrome-molybdenum steel alloy, typical of those that had been produced by the Western industrial nations since the end of the First World War. The scheme of application of armour followed closely that of *Baden*, with thicker horizontal and somewhat thinner vertical protection. The side armour was in two tiers, the upper tier extending downwards from the forecastle-deck with a uniform thickness of 5.7in(145mm); the main belt, two decks deep and protecting the waterline, was 10.6in(270mm) thick where it met the upper tier, increased to 12.6in(320mm) on the waterline and then tapered to 6.7in(170mm) at its lower edge. This distribution and thickness did not compare particularly favourably with the vertical armour of the other modern European battleships, all of which had thicker main belts—*Richelieu* had 8.8in(225mm) above 15.75in (400mm) and *King George V* had between 14in(356mm) and 15in(380mm) in three tiers, the lowest tapering to $4\frac{1}{2}$in(114mm) and $5\frac{1}{2}$in(140mm), with a total height of 23ft 6in(7.2m). The German upper tier was of little protective value against heavy shells, and even the main belt would have been defeated by 15in(380mm) projectiles fired from within about 17,000yds(15,550m)

and striking at 90° ('normal') inclination. Of course, shells fired at this range would not arrive at 90° to the armour, and as the angle decreased, so the effective thickness of the plate increased.

With the improvements in post-war gunnery control, permitting firing at very long range, more attention had to be paid to protection against projectiles arriving at angles of descent in excess of 20°, known as 'plunging fire', on the deck instead of on the side of the ship. In general, shells striking on deck at inclinations of less than 20°, were likely to pass over magazines and much of the machinery, but with accurate shooting possible at over 25,000yds(22,800m), inclinations of up to 35° became possible, necessitating deck protection against shell instead of merely shell splinters. Fortunately, the angle of striking was such that about 6 inches(150mm) of plate was sufficient to withstand a 1,940lb(882kg) shell fired at a range of more than 30,000yds(28,000m). Aircraft bombs had emerged as a potential ship-killing weapon, and although their weight and terminal velocity were less than those of shells in 1939, their angle of impact was near vertical and 1,000lb(500kg) bombs dropped from above 15,000ft(4,500m) would penetrate 6in(152mm) armour: the probability of such a hit on a moving target was much less than airmen claimed or seamen feared.

In 1927, the Royal Navy accepted two new battleships with the first armour scheme designed to defeat plunging shell. *Nelson* and *Rodney* had an 'all-or-nothing' concentration of armour over magazines and machinery, two decks below the forecastle level, but above the waterline; the side armour belt extended downwards from the sides of this one armoured deck, while armour bulkheads forward and aft, closed off the ends to form a bottomless box. The French Navy improved on this scheme in the *Dunkerque* class, raising the armoured deck one level higher, and inserting a thinner layer of armour immediately over the machinery and magazines to stop any splinters or spalls from the higher deck. The succeeding *Richelieu* class went further by way of increasing the thickness of the upper-deck armour from 4.9in(125mm) to 5.1in (130mm) over the machinery, and 6.7in(170mm) over magazines and shell rooms, and reducing the thickness of the lower anti-splinter deck to 1.5in(40mm). In the *King George V* class, the Royal Navy took the armoured deck up to the level below the forecastle, providing 6in(152mm) over the magazines and 5in(127mm) over the machinery. The *Littorio* had a similar scheme, a deck lower than in the British and French ships, with 5.8in(150mm) over the magazines and 3.9in(100mm) above the machinery, outboard of which, the deck thinned to 3.5in(90mm); this relationship was reversed in *North Carolina*, which had 3.4in(88mm) over the machinery and 4in(102mm) extending outboard to meet the top of the 11.25in(285.7mm)-thick waterline belt, well above the waterline.

It was in the distribution of horizontal armour that *Tirpitz* and *Bismarck* fell so far behind their contemporaries, for apart from the improvement in material quality, the only improvement upon *Baden* was the addition of an armoured deck near the waterline, flat over the magazines and machinery spaces and angled downwards 25° to meet the lower edge of the belt; the flat armour was 3.15in(80mm) thick over the engine and boiler rooms and 3.9in(100mm) over the magazines. The inclined armour was 4.3in(110mm) thick, and was set at an angle primarily in order to join the flat to the bottom of the vertical armour, for its protective value was limited to stopping shells hitting and defeating the main belt on or near the waterline. The German battleship armour was, therefore, in the form of a box with a moderately thick floor and it was provided with a lid, in the form of the 1.97in(50mm) armoured forecastle-deck, stretching from the cable-holders forward, right aft to the quarterdeck. *Tirpitz* thus had a total thickness of armour of 5.9in(150mm) and 5.1in (130mm)—comparable to that of *King George V*. But one thick layer of armour is more resistant to penetration than two layers of the same total thickness, partly because the upper layer will tend to deflect the projectile downwards at a steeper angle, thereby reducing the effective thickness of the deck below. The upper deck in *Tirpitz* would have scarcely been proof against plunging 6in(152mm) shells—it was not proof against 500lb(227kg) Semi-Armour-Piercing bombs released from above 3,000ft(900m)—and therefore the entire volume of the ship above the waterline was vulnerable to shells and bombs, with the exception of the turrets and their barbettes. Although such damage would not let in sufficient water to cause the ship's loss, most of the essential fighting services—including manoeuvring and fire-control communications—ran through the ill-protected sections for at least part of their length.

This serious weakness in the design was dramatically proved on two occasions. In the final action with *Rodney* and *King George V*, most of the hits were scored at too close a range for the British 14in(356mm) and 16in(406mm) shells to strike at any great angle of inclination, so that the strength of the main armoured deck was not greatly tested. A very few hits caused virtually complete loss of communications at an early stage, and by the end of the action, *Bismarck* was wrecked from end to end above the waterline and required only three torpedo hits to sink her. Three years later, *Tirpitz* was hit by 14 aircraft bombs, none

of which exploded below the armoured deck, but which disrupted communications and inflicted severe personnel casualties above that level, although only five bombs exploded below the 1.97in(50mm) armour of the upper-deck.

The main armament turret armour was appreciably thicker than that in *King George V*, the front face having 14.2in(360mm), compared with 12.75in(324mm), but the barbettes which supported the gun-houses and protected the ammunition hoists were only 8.7in (220mm) thick, 3.3in(85mm) less than *King George V*'s thinnest barbette armour. The fore- and after-most turrets—'Anton' and 'Dora'—were at forecastle level, so that their barbettes were adequately covered by the 2.2in(55mm) deck armour and the 5.7in(145mm) upper belt, but the barbettes of the superfiring turrets —'Bruno' and 'Caesar'—were exposed to a height of some 15ft(4.6m) above the forecastle. The total weight of fixed armour (excluding gun-houses, conning tower and directors) was 17,263.8 tons, compared with 12,500 tons in *King George V*, approximately 14,000 tons in *Richelieu* and 13,453 tons in *Littorio*.

Internal sub-division was extensive, although the major compartments were larger than those in *Baden*. However, total watertight integrity below the main armoured deck was sacrificed to convenience of access between sections, numerous doors piercing the transverse bulkheads on the platform-decks. Although the doors were watertight, they could not be made proof against opening by shock, and there was thus a real risk of widespread flooding if the ship were to sustain serious underwater damage.

The main armament consisted of eight 380mm(15in) Seekanone c/34 guns of 47 calibres bore length (47 x 380mm = 58ft 9in), mounted in four Lafette c/34 rotating, elevating mountings. In its characteristics, the gun was very similar to the 380mm(15in) 50-cal guns designed in Italy and France in 1934 and 1935, the longer barrels of the other guns being intended to preserve the high muzzle velocity with a heavier projectile:

	max eleva- tion	muzzle velocity	max range*	shell weight
German 15in(380mm)	30°	2690fps (820m/s)	39,600yds (36,200m)	1,760lb (800kg)
French 15in(380mm)	30°	2690fps (820m/s)	38,300yds (35,000m)	1,945lb (884kg)
Italian 15in(380mm)	35°	2850fps (870m/s)	46,800yds (42,800m)	1,947lb (885kg)
British 14in(356mm)	40°	2475fps (754m/s)	36,000yds (32,900m)	1,590lb (723kg)

* Note: The range quoted is the maximum for which the guns were sighted, except for the Italian 15in(380mm), where maximum gun range is quoted, regardless of sighting and calibration restrictions.

The German claims for the penetration against face-hardened plate indicate that the armour-piercing qualities of the L/4.4 shell were exceptional—13.8in (350mm) at 22,000yds(20,100m), at 20° angle of inclination. This was more than the thickness penetrable by the 1937-model shell used by the old British 15in(380mm) gun and utterly beyond the capabilities of the new British 14in(356mm). *King George V*'s only gunnery advantages were that the guns fired slightly faster (2 rounds per minute against 1.5rpm) and the broadside weight was greater, so that after six minutes she would have expended 85 tons of projectiles, whereas *Tirpitz* would have fired only 56 tons, or, 120 14in(356mm) shells to 72 380mm(15in) shells.

The number of shells fired, however, was not so important as the number of hits scored, a factor dependent upon the accuracy and reliability of the fire-control systems. Although the German optical range-finding equipment was still superior to that in all other navies, by the time that *Bismarck* and *Tirpitz* became operational, the Royal Navy had established a lead in radar range-finding. *Bismarck* was hit by *Rodney*'s third salvo during the action on 27 May 1941, and on 26 December 1943, *Duke of York* hit *Scharnhorst* with her first salvo—in both cases, the guns were laid on ranges obtained from Type 284 50cm wavelength radar, which could detect the shell splashes and even shells in flight, outbound and inbound. The Funk-messortung 25 and 26 (FuMO 25 and 26) Seetakt 'Gema' radar fitted to all three of the directors which controlled both the main and the secondary batteries in *Tirpitz* did not possess such discrimination, partly because of its slightly longer wavelength (80cm) and its considerably broader radiated beam, but mainly because German naval electronics technology did not develop sufficiently quickly, despite a commanding lead in 1939, to provide the necessary sophisticated 'circuitry' and display units. Thus, by 1944, when a *King George V* class battleship had separate fire-control radars for main, dual-purpose and close-range weapons, as well as separate navigational and air warning/control sets, *Tirpitz* still had only her three 'Gema' sets for all warning and control purposes.

The German concept of a secondary battery intended for surface action was outdated, although the Italian and Japanese Navies also gave their new battleships such a battery. The six twin turrets and their magazines had to be armoured, and took up a volume hardly commensurate with their value in action, whether against torpedo-firing destroyers or, in poorly-controlled barrage fire, against aircraft. The French Navy elected to install a dual-purpose secondary battery of nine 152mm(6in) guns which were genuine anti-aircraft weapons as well as being capable of fire against ship targets in the astern sector, not covered by the main armament turrets, but retained a tertiary battery of heavy AA guns.

In *Tirpitz*, the heavy AA armament consisted of four 4.1in(105mm) twin mountings on either side of the superstructure, controlled by four tri-axially stabilised directors located one on each side of the bridge structure, one immediately abaft the main mast and one immediately forward of 'c' turret. The guns were fast-firing and had an excellent performance, but there was no overhead protection for the guns' crews on the mounting, and serious casualties were sustained from strafing fighters. The British and American naval staffs opted for a dual-purpose secondary battery whose main purpose was AA defence. While the US Navy used the standard destroyer-type 5in(127mm) 38-cal gun, the Royal Navy decided to install the 5.25in(133.3mm) gun, in order to retain a heavier gun than that fitted to most destroyers; in consequence, only eight twin turrets could be incorporated, compared with ten in *North Carolina*, and the gun was rather too slow-firing and the mounting's rate of training was too slow due to its weight (manual training of the turret after a power failure was not really practical in action against aircraft).

The original close-range Flak armament consisted of eight 37mm twin and sixteen 20mm single mountings. The 37mm twin mounting was peculiar to the navy, and was stabilised against pitch, roll and the corkscrew motion produced by the combination of the first two; the 37mm guns were the standard Rheinmetall weapons used by the other arms of the Wehrmacht, with a high rate of fire in bursts, getting off an eight-round clip in three seconds but with an equal 'dead time' spent re-loading between clips, so that the practical rate of fire was 80 rounds per minute per barrel; maximum useful anti-aircraft range was of the order of 5,500yds (5,000m), but as all control was from the mounting, the effective range was rather less. The sixteen 20mm Rheinmetall guns were of the standard Wehrmacht Flak 30 pattern—a high-velocity weapon with a useful range of about 3,000yds(2,750m), but with a 'dead time' which reduced the rate of fire from a cyclic (mechanically possible) 280 rounds per minute, to 120 rounds per minute achieved. The German 20mm's superiority over the faster-firing single-barrel Oerlikon used by the Allies lay partly in its higher muzzle velocity, but more in the nature of the mounting, the gun being rigidly mounted in a cradle which was elevated and traversed by means of hand-wheels; the Oerlikon, in its single-barrel form, was laid by a gunner who was strapped into a harness attached to the gun itself, and whose aim suffered as a result of the vibration of firing.

Tirpitz's light flak armament was progressively improved by the addition of faster-firing (c.200rpm) Flak 38 guns on quadruple (Vierling) fully-stabilized mountings. Eventually, *Tirpitz* boasted 16 of these mountings, each capable of firing over 800 rounds per minute, installed on top of 'B' and 'C' turrets, on two of the 150mm(5.9in) turrets, in place of the searchlights on either side of the funnel, and on any available flat space around the superstructure. By early 1944, *Tirpitz* could bring nine single and nine quadruple 20mm guns to bear on either beam, with a total rate of fire of over 8,500 rounds per minute.

An unusual armament 'fit' for the day was the installation of two sets of quadruple torpedo tubes on the upper deck, abreast the after superstructure. A full set of reloads was carried, giving *Tirpitz* sixteen 21in (533mm) G7a steam torpedoes, intended for use against targets found on raiding cruises. No other modern battleship was thus armed (including *Bismarck*), although several of the older vessels were armed with tubes.

The aircraft arrangements in *Tirpitz* differed slightly from those in *Bismarck*. Whereas the latter had hangarage for one aircraft on each side of the funnel, and a double hangar capable of holding four aircraft at the base of the mainmast, *Tirpitz* had two single-aircraft hangars in the latter position, reducing her maximum capacity from six to four floatplanes. These were Arado Ar 196A monoplanes, intended for use on reconnaissance missions, rather than as spotters in a fleet action. With an endurance of about four hours, they had a radius of action of 175 nautical miles(320km) and a maximum speed at low level of 165 knots (305km/h), so that they were appreciably faster than the Royal Navy's and French Navy's catapult aircraft, and the former's biplane torpedo-bombers. A double-action athwartships catapult was fitted, the aircraft being launched from a trolley into a relative wind which was a resultant of the actual wind and the ship's speed through the water. Two seaplane cranes were fitted, one on each beam, to recover the aircraft from the water and to handle the ship's larger boats.

The total weight of armament was 6,120 tons, exclusive of ammunition, which came to a further 1,480 tons. *King George V*'s initial armament weight was 6,567 tons, with 834 tons of ammunition: the latter figure increased during the war, as outfits for close-range armament were increased to meet the requirements established by hard experience. *Littorio*'s total armament weight was 6,460 tons—compared with *Tirpitz*, she had an extra 380mm(15in) gun at a penalty of only 340 tons, thanks to the use of triple turrets. Perhaps the most surprisingly economical (in terms of weight) armament was also the most powerful —that of *North Carolina*, in which the three 16in (406mm) triple turrets and their armour, the ten 5in(127mm) twin mountings and the original close-range armament totalled only 5,700 tons.*

Inevitably, the standard displacement of the German battleships was far in excess of the 35,000 tons permitted by the 1935 Anglo-German Naval Agreement, the 41,700 tons amounting to an increase of 19 per cent. No subsequent Treaty or Agreement modified the limitation in Germany's favour, contrary to what has been said elsewhere, but an offer by Britain in late 1938 to raise the limit to 40,000 tons was summarily dismissed by Germany, on the grounds that the latter did not wish to be restricted at all.

In fairness to Germany, it must be pointed out that none of the '35,000-ton' battleships remained within limits:

King George V	36,700 tons	5 per cent excess
North Carolina	36,450 tons	4 per cent excess
Richelieu	38,500 tons	10 per cent excess
Littorio	37,205 tons**	6 per cent excess

At full load, however, *Tirpitz* became one of the 'all-time greats', her 1944 deep displacement of 52,660 tons being exceeded only by the four US Navy ships of the *Iowa* class and the two Japanese ships, *Yamato* and *Musashi*.

The contract for the construction of Schlachtschiff 'G', the replacement for the 1906 pre-dreadnought *Schleswig Holstein*, was awarded to the Naval Yard (Marinewerft), Wilhelmshaven, in the opening months of 1936, but the keel could not be laid on the only adequate slipway until it had been vacated by the hull of *Scharnhorst*. The latter was launched on 3 October 1936 and three weeks later, on 24 October, 'G' was laid down.

She spent 29 months on the ways before she was launched on 1 April 1939 by Frau von Hassel, the grand-daughter of Admiral Alfred von Tirpitz, the architect of the Imperial German Fleet which had encouraged Kaiser Wilhelm II in his ambitions for a worldwide Empire to the extent that he believed that he could challenge the naval might of the British Empire. Tirpitz had given Germany a big ship navy to fight on the oceans—it was ironic that the ship named for him should spend its life lurking in coastal waters. The Commander-in-Chief of the *Kriegsmarine*, Erich

* Raven and Roberts, *British Battleships of World War Two*, (Arms & Armour Press, 1976), p. 409 fn.
** Giorgerini and Nani, *Le Navi di Linea Italiane*, (Ufficio Storico della Marina Militare, 1962), p. 251. (The usual figure quoted, 41,782 tonnes, is the trials displacement.)

Raeder, was promoted Grossadmiral (equivalent to a Field Marshal) on the occasion of *Tirpitz*'s launching, which was a major political event, attended by Hitler and the National Socialist hierarchy.

Machinery trials were carried out in the fitting-out basin as early as April 1940, but she was not completed and ready for sea trials until 25 February 1941, having commissioned on 23 December 1941. *Tirpitz* left Wilhelmshaven for Kiel, via the Kaiser Wilhelm Canal, to begin trials in the safe waters of the Baltic. Kiel remained the base port for several months, visits also being made to Gdynia and Gotenhafen (Danzig), and her movements were followed by agents and Royal Air Force reconnaissance aircraft. The RAF also attempted to bomb her in dry dock at Kiel on a number of occasions, but no hits were made on the ship and very few on the dockyard. Gunnery trials off Rugen Island in June 1941 showed up defects which kept her in harbour throughout July and August; not until 20 September 1941 did she carry out the final successful shoots, after which, she was ready for operations.

2

'To Norroway, to Norroway'

The sinking of *Bismarck* on 27 May 1941 did not entirely shake the conviction of the German Naval Staff (the Seekriegsleitung—SKL) that individual heavy surface units could disrupt the British ocean convoy system while themselves running minimal risks. Hitler, the C-in-C of all the German armed forces, directed that any future raiding foray was not to be undertaken if there were any possibility of the loss of a capital ship. This directive was to govern and circumscribe the entire career of *Tirpitz*, from September 1941, when she sailed for her first cautious operation, until September 1944, when British aircraft destroyed her capability for sea operations.

Notwithstanding the directive, the SKL ordered the pocket battleship *Lützow* to Trondheim in June 1941, to prepare for a raiding cruise in the North Atlantic. She did not reach Trondheim, however, for on 13 June she was torpedoed south of Lindesnes by a Bristol Beaufort of No 114 Squadron RAF, and she had to return to Kiel for repairs. Hitler had counselled against the operation, and the SKL was accordingly poorly placed when it came to proposing, in early September, that *Tirpitz*, together with the heavy cruiser *Admiral Hipper*, should be transferred to Brest from the Baltic in order to concentrate the surface fleet at a base from which it could operate effectively against Allied shipping without first having to skirt around the breakwater formed by the British Isles and the minefields which extended from the Shetlands to Iceland. What was to have been a carbon copy of the *Bismarck* operation plan was vetoed by Hitler who was fully supported in this instance by the new Flag-Officer, Battleships, Vice-Admiral O. Ciliax, and the Flag-Officers of Groups North and West, all of whom feared a repetition of the end of *Bismarck*'s mission more than they desired a concentration at Brest.

Meanwhile, the war had taken on a new dimension with the invasion of Russia on 22 June 1941. The Baltic had become a war zone, although German naval superiority was never seriously challenged by the Soviet Fleet, whose main base was at Kronstadt, at the head of the Gulf of Finland. By mid-September, the Baltic coast was almost entirely controlled by German forces, and the city of Leningrad was under siege by the end of that month. *Tirpitz*'s first operation took place between 26 and 29 September when, accompanied by the pocket battleship *Admiral Scheer,* light cruisers, destroyers, torpedo-boats and minesweepers, she stood by off the Åland Islands to guard against a possible sortie by the Soviet Fleet. The latter remained in harbour until 1944.

Following this operation, the SKL recommended that *Tirpitz* and *Hipper* be transferred to Norway, where they could be of material assistance to the Russian Front by intercepting the eastbound 'PQ' convoys which were carrying supplies from Britain to north Russia. The first of forty such convoys had sailed in August 1941, starting from Iceland and arriving at Archangel and Murmansk. The German heavy units would also serve as a deterrent against the Royal Navy's attacks on German coastal convoys in Norwegian waters. Hitler approved of the plans: since a British Commando raid on the Lofoten Islands in March 1941, he had become convinced that Britain intended to mount a full-scale invasion of Norway.

Norway was of extreme economic and military importance to Germany. High-grade iron ore from the Gällivare area in Sweden, supplying virtually all Germany's vast war production needs, could be shipped all the year round from Narvik, in northern Norway. Although the Baltic route was shorter, and completely free from danger of British attack, the Swedish port of Lulea, which also served Gällivare, was icebound throughout the winter and spring. Another vital import was Finnish nickel, brought from the northern ice-free port of Petsamo (now Pechenga and in the USSR). Militarily, Norway served as a jumping-off point for the invasion of northern Russia, which had as its main objective the port of Murmansk, and the numerous fiords provided bases for German warships, by-passing the breakwater formed across the North Sea by the British Isles.

The German forces allocated to the capture of Murmansk were not strong enough, and spirited Russian counter-attacks brought the Arctic invasion to a standstill within a month. The vital Anglo-Russian link was thus preserved, and Hitler became increasingly pre-occupied with the possibility of a British invasion of Norway.

In spite of this anxiety, Hitler, who had said at one of his Conferences in December 1941, 'Every ship that is not in Norway is in the wrong place', refused to sanction the planned move of *Tirpitz* until assured by the SKL that she could arrive undamaged. On 12 January 1942, *Tirpitz* left Kiel and proceeded through the Kaiser Wilhelm Canal to Wilhelmshaven, whence she sailed on the night of 14/15 January, arriving at Trondheim on 16 January. In this way, *Tirpitz* avoided the passage of the Great Belt, between Denmark and Sweden; it was believed that previous movements through these narrow waters had been reported to Britain by agents in Sweden. On this occasion, the ploy was undoubtedly successful, for British air reconnaissance did not locate *Tirpitz* until a week after her arrival at Trondheim—a frightening failure for the Allies, for in that time she could have reached Brest to join the battlecruisers.

Instead, it had been decided that the battlecruisers would join her, and a month after *Tirpitz* reached Trondheim, *Scharnhorst*, *Gneisenau* and the cruiser *Prinz Eugen* broke out of Brest and stormed through the English Channel to reach Wilhelmshaven. Both battlecruisers were damaged by mines laid by aircraft, but again the RAF had failed to observe the movement in time.

On 21 February, amends were made when a reconnaissance aircraft sighted *Prinz Eugen* and *Admiral Scheer* northbound off the Danish coast, following *Tirpitz*'s route to Trondheim. An attempt to trap the German force enjoyed only partial success: RAF torpedo-bombers failed to locate the ships, a search by Fairey Albacore torpedo-bombers from the carrier *Victorious* passed through the correct area, but in bad weather, and the submarine *Trident* alone made successful contact, blowing *Prinz Eugen*'s rudders off and inflicting severe damage to the extreme aft end. The arrival of *Scheer* and five undamaged destroyers at Trondheim was, however, of considerable importance to German plans.

Tirpitz had been virtually immobilised at Trondheim since her arrival, because the destroyers which provided her anti-submarine and reconnaissance screen had been sent to Brest to escort the battlecruisers home. The battleship had thus been unable to sortie against convoy PQ8 at the end of January, and would have been unable to operate against PQ9, 10, or 11, had these convoys been located by German reconnaissance. Although Hitler had ordered that the Luftwaffe in Norway was to be reinforced to provide a comprehensive maritime reconnaissance and strike force, the units required had not yet been transferred, and there were, as yet, less than a dozen long-range search aircraft available, with a similar number of long-range strike aircraft.

3

Operation 'Sportpalast'

On 5 March 1942, German reconnaissance aircraft made their first major contribution in these waters by sighting convoy PQ12 to the south of Jan Mayen Land. The ocean escort consisted of the light cruiser *Kenya* and two destroyers, but in support was the Home Fleet, with the battleships *King George V*, *Duke of York*, the battlecruiser *Renown*, a heavy cruiser, and the aircraft carrier *Victorious*. This force was cruising independently, within 100 miles of the convoy, but was not discovered until 7 March. Meanwhile, the German Flag-Officer, Group North, had requested permission to sail *Tirpitz* and *Scheer* against PQ12. The SKL delayed, and when permission was granted on 6 March, it was for *Tirpitz* and three destroyers only, on the grounds that *Scheer* was too slow to operate in company. *Tirpitz*, flying the flag of Vice-Admiral Ciliax, sailed from Trondheim at noon on 6 March for her first offensive operation—'Sportpalast' (Sports Stadium).

For the second time in three weeks, the RAF failed to notice a vitally important German surface ship leave harbour. The regular daily reconnaissance sortie failed to show *Tirpitz*'s departure, and the special offshore patrol for the benefit of PQ12 was cancelled. Fortunately, the submarines *Trident* and *Seawolf* sighted her and the destroyers *Z.25*, *Hermann Schoemann*, and *Friedrich Ihn* as they left the northern approaches to Trondheim at about 1700 on 6 March. Neither submarine was close enough to attempt an attack, nor even to distinguish the identity of the big ship, but *Seawolf* sent an alerting signal to the Admiralty, who in turn passed it on to Admiral Sir John Tovey, C-in-C Home Fleet.

Tirpitz headed north to intercept PQ12. No further sighting reports of the convoy had been received, and the original report had underestimated the convoy's speed by two knots. The weather was poor, with drizzle and snow showers, so that *Tirpitz* did not launch her two Arado Ar 196A floatplanes to search for PQ12; instead, Admiral Ciliax detached his three destroyers to search to the north-north-west while

Tirpitz searched to the north-west—astern of the estimated position of the convoy. The weather probably saved *Tirpitz* from detection, for at 1000 on 7 March, an hour after the German destroyers had been detached, *Victorious* was to have flown off a search covering an easterly quadrant to a depth of 120 miles. At this time, *Tirpitz* was 110 miles east-south-east of the Home Fleet, heading into the planned search sector, and the three destroyers were about 25 miles north of *Tirpitz* and 95 miles south-east of PQ12. The severe icing conditions resulted in the cancellation of the search, and the Home Fleet later turned away to find better flying conditions. At noon, the two convoys —PQ12 and the returning QP8—passed through each other in a snowstorm which reduced visibility to less than a mile.

Two hours after this unplanned manoeuvre, the easternmost German destroyer, *Z.25*, passed less than 10 miles ahead of QP8, but both sides remained unaware of the near encounter. At 1545, *Z.25* did sight smoke to the north: this proved to be from the Russian freighter *Ijora*, which had straggled from QP8. *Ijora* sent a distress signal, with an accurate position, at 1632, but *Friedrich Ihn* did not manage to finish her off until 1715, as *Tirpitz* came up to the scene. This was the closest to an Allied surface vessel that the battleship ever came during her career. She was, at this time, 75 miles north-west of PQ12, with the Home Fleet about 150 miles to the south-west. The German Navy was completely unaware of the presence of the Home Fleet, or of the positions of the two convoys, but the Home Fleet had been alerted by *Ijora*'s sos, and a subsequent wireless transmission from the German warships, which provided the Fleet's high-frequency direction finders with a bearing on the enemy.

Admiral Tovey was not certain that the transmission came from a German heavy unit and so split his force, sending the six destroyers of the 17th Destroyer Flotilla to sweep across and along the direct track, from *Ijora*'s last position to Trondheim, while the heavy ships, with only one destroyer, headed for a covering position off Bear Island. The decision to despatch the destroyers was reinforced by another D/F bearing which suggested that an enemy unit was returning to the south at high speed. This, in fact, was *Friedrich Ihn*, proceeding to Tromsö to refuel. *Tirpitz* and the remaining pair of destroyers headed east during the night, in order to reach a position to the south-east of Bear Island, from which, to begin another search. Not until the late evening of 7 March, did Admiral Ciliax learn that the Home Fleet was at sea, although no information as to its position was available.

The unescorted Home Fleet turned back to the south at midnight on 7/8 March: Admiral Tovey, without a destroyer screen, did not wish to enter a probable U-boat operating area off Bear Island, and he wanted to be able to support the detached destroyers from dawn. By 0400, he was 80 miles to the west of the 17th Destroyer Flotilla, which, in turn, was 200 miles south-west of *Tirpitz*. At the same time, the German battleship detached *Z.25* and *Hermann Schoemann* to Tromsö to refuel. PQ12 was only 90 miles to the north-west, heading for the ice-edge to the west of Bear Island, well to the north of its planned track, and even farther to the north of the track predicted for it by Group North.

As a result, the three main participants—*Tirpitz*, PQ12, and the Home Fleet—were in total ignorance of each other's positions for the next 16 hours. *Tirpitz* ran to the west and was never closer than 55 miles to the convoy, while the Home Fleet steered towards Iceland at 24 knots, intending to collect some fully-fuelled destroyers before returning to the north. In this, Admiral Tovey was being assisted by the Admiralty, which had ordered four cruisers to two positions 190 miles south and east of Jan Mayen Land, to act as 'filling stations' for the destroyers being collected in Iceland, Scapa Flow, Rosyth, and Loch Ewe. At 1820, the Home Fleet again turned to the north-east, intending to sweep between Bear Island and the Norwegian coast. For the first time, Admiral Tovey broke wireless silence, to inform the Admiralty of his intention and to tell them that he was without a destroyer screen.

This message went undetected by the German D/F stations, but a signal from *Tirpitz* four minutes earlier did not elude the British organisation. Admiral Ciliax had been informed that Group North believed that because PQ12 had not been sighted since 5 March, it was possible that it had turned back! Admiral Ciliax's acknowledgement presented the Home Fleet with a welcome bearing. Two hours later, with *Tirpitz* steaming south, a signal from Ciliax to the destroyers

at Tromsö, ordering them to rendezvous with him off the Lofoten Islands gave yet another bearing, which indicated that a German unit was moving south. The Home Fleet therefore, headed towards the Lofotens, increasing to 26 knots in the early hours of 9 March, in order to launch a search from *Victorious* soon after dawn.

Victorious had taken part in the hunt for *Bismarck* in May 1941, and although, on that occasion, her strike aircraft had been embarked for only three days, and neither the ship nor the squadron were fully worked-up, the Swordfish of 825 Squadron had obtained a torpedo hit. Now she was fully worked-up and her two Albacore squadrons had been embarked throughout the winter of 1941/42. 817 and 832 Squadrons had taken part in the night search for *Admiral Scheer* in February, but unfortunately, the Commanding Officer of 832 Squadron had been lost during the operation; furthermore, a new CO had taken over 817 Squadron shortly before the ship had sailed to cover PQ12. Neither of the new COs had an opportunity to lead even a practice strike before being called upon to attack *Tirpitz*, and although their pilots had made numerous dummy attacks, there had been an acute shortage of practice 'runner' torpedoes—torpedoes with ballast in place of a warhead, and which gave an accurate indication of proficiency.

At this date, the Royal Navy's torpedo attack tactics were quite unique, but had been in vogue for nearly ten years. Appreciating that naval aircraft were slow, and therefore good gunnery targets, the tactics developed posed the most difficult fire-control problems possible with the aircraft available. Approaching at medium level—generally at about 6,000–9,000ft(1,800–2,750m) —the strike formation would deploy into attack formation when ahead of the target, and dive steeply to less than 200ft(61m) above the water, levelling out within a mile of the target and releasing at 1,000 yards(900m) or less. Attacking in sub-flights of three aircraft, the later groups would be able to adjust their aim according to the direction of the target's evasive manoeuvres. The maximum permissible ground-speed for the release of the Mark XII 18in(457mm) torpedo was 150 knots, from a height of less than 200ft(61m), so that speed was not a factor to be considered in survival, which depended upon giving the enemy gunnery control widely separated targets with high angular rates of change of bearing until the last half-mile, when the aircraft were low down on the water, with the pilots making their final aiming corrections.

The Fairey Albacore was a multi-purpose torpedo-bomber-reconnaissance biplane, designed in 1936, and in service during the summer of 1940. Compared to the earlier Swordfish, it was a much improved aircraft. In order to take the maximum advantage of the 1,010hp Bristol Taurus engine, considerable attention had been paid to aerodynamic refinement. Maximum level speed was 155 knots, or about 130 knots with a torpedo, and to keep the speed down to the torpedo-release limits during the approach dive, the Albacore boasted dive-brakes. The pilot's cockpit was ahead of the wing leading edges, and the pilot's head was in line with the upper mainplane, so that he had an excellent view for attack and for deck-landing. The Observer and Telegraphist-Air Gunner shared a roomy cockpit behind the wings; both cockpits were fully enclosed. Considerable difficulty had been experienced in fitting air-to-surface vessel radar (ASV) to the Albacore, and only half a dozen on board *Victorious* were so equipped.

At 0645 on 9 March, three Albacores from each squadron were flown off from a position 170 miles to the north-west of the entrance to Vestfjord, the main approach to Narvik, on a search planned to cover a 50° sector to the east and south-east, out to a distance of 150 miles. The visibility was very good between snow showers, but the general cloud base was at 2,000ft (600m) and airframe and engine icing was to be expected in cloud at all heights. The wind was from the north-east—a stiff 35 knots—giving the enemy the 'weather gauge', an advantage as great in these days of aircraft as it had been in the days of sail.

As soon as the search aircraft had left, twelve Albacores—seven from 832 and five from 817—were ranged on deck, armed with torpedoes. This strike was flown off at 0735, led by Lieutenant-Commander W. J. Lucas, RN, the CO of 832 Squadron. The Albacores flew out on a south-easterly track, following the track of Sub-Lieutenant (A) T. T. Miller, RN, in T9215, Albacore 'F' of 832 Squadron.

When the search was flown off, *Tirpitz* had been 115 miles to the east-south-east of the Home Fleet heading direct for Trondheim, and *Friedrich Ihn* rejoined her at 0650. At 0800, when only 70 miles south-east of the Home Fleet, *Tirpitz* was sighted by the crew of '4-F', and a first brief sighting report was transmitted at 0803: 'One BS 160'.* Subsequent amplifying reports were relayed via Albacore '4-L', which acted as a communications link with *Victorious*, while two other Albacores—'H' of 832 and 'F' of 817—also took up shadowing positions, at 0845 and 0816 respectively. *Tirpitz* had sighted '4-F' at 0815 and Admiral Ciliax realised that it would be only a matter of time before a torpedo strike arrived. He therefore decided to turn and run for the shelter of Vestfjord and Narvik, the entrance to the former being only 50 miles

* ('One battleship bearing 160° from the Fleet')

to the east. Before the ship turned, however, a single Arado Ar 196A was launched to drive off the shadower.

The striking force had received the initial sighting reports and subsequent position reports from '4-F' and '5-F', including the battleship's change of course at 0832. At 0842, Lieutenant-Commander Lucas sighted *Tirpitz* at a range of 20 miles, and three minutes later, he led the formation up to 3,500ft (1,050m) from the 500ft(150m) at which the strike had approached. Coming in below the radar horizon until the sighting, the Albacores were now closing *Tirpitz* in cloud, using ASV radar to track the target. The cloud cover and ASV were the Albacores' only advantages, for *Tirpitz* was heading at 26 knots into a 35-knot wind, and the aircraft were approaching at their best cruising speed of 90 knots, so that they had a closing rate of only a mile every two minutes! The icing conditions added a further handicap and in order to give the formation more freedom of manoeuvre, Lucas ordered the other three sub-flights to 'act independently', thus opening the intervals between the groups of three.

Meanwhile, *Tirpitz*'s attention was being distracted by '4-F'. At 0845, the Ar 196A made the first of several unsuccessful interceptions. On each occasion, the Albacore took refuge in the cloud and only once did Leading Airman Lindley, the TAG, have to open fire with his twin Vickers 'K' machine-guns, claiming to have damaged the Arado in the empennage. The same floatplane also approached '4-H', at 08.55, and then used up the last of its ammunition on X9138, 'K' of 817 Squadron. Hits were scored on '5-K' and the Observer, Sub-Lieutenant (A) G. Dunworth, RNVR, was wounded in the legs. In spite of his wounds, Dunworth continued to navigate, shadowing and reporting *Tirpitz* until the torpedo strike was delivered.

At 0917, the strike reached a break in the clouds. *Tirpitz* was less than a mile away from Lucas's sub-flight, and almost abeam, to starboard; the other three sub-flights were all to starboard of the target—ill-placed, if Lucas should attack first and *Tirpitz* should turn to port to avoid the first torpedoes. *Tirpitz* did not open fire immediately, although *Friedrich Ihn* did, and Lucas decided to attack immediately, believing that he might surprise *Tirpitz*, and knowing that if the attack were delayed while the strike worked ahead of the ships, it would be made against fully-prepared guns' crews.

At 0918, the leading sub-flight ('4-A, -B, -C') dived to attack, turning to starboard to release three torpedoes broad on *Tirpitz*'s port bow at 0920½. The range at release, was 1,900 yards(1,740m) to intersection with *Tirpitz*'s track; the closest of the 40-knot torpedoes crossed about 20 seconds—150 yards—astern of the target. As a result of the independent manoeuvring in cloud during the approach, the next sub-flight to starboard was the second of 817 Squadron—'5M', '-H' and '4-G'. These three aircraft crossed over to the port side of *Tirpitz*'s track, to cover possible evading action by the battleship in that direction, leaving the second sub-flight of 832, and the first of 817 to deal with an evading turn to starboard. *Tirpitz* duly turned to port, but the leader of the sub-flight underestimated the distance his torpedo would have to run to intersect the battleship's track and, as a result, all three torpedoes dropped at 0921½ passed well astern. The six aircraft of these first two sub-flights disengaged without suffering damage.

Having evaded the first wave's attack, *Tirpitz* turned back to starboard, so completing an 's-turn'. The other two sub-flights had managed to work ahead, assisted by the battleship's 'jink' to port, which had allowed them to cut the corner. By 0925½, when all six released their torpedoes, the Albacores were spread in a 45° fan centred on *Tirpitz*. The ranges at release varied between 2,000 yards(1,830m) and 1,000 yards(900m), although the Germans estimated the minimum range as 450 yards(400m). One torpedo—probably '5-L' 's—passed only 10 yards(9.1m) from the starboard quarter but the others passed well clear. As the Albacores disengaged, with the wind behind them, several strafed the battleship's bridge and unprotected flak mountings, wounding three gunners. Two aircraft—'5-C' (X9020) of 817 Squadron, flown by Sub-Lieutenant R. C. Jones, RNVR, with Leading Airman Sivewright as TAG, and '4-P' (T9210) of 832 Squadron, flown by Sub-Lieutenant D. J. Shephard, RNVR, with Sub-Lieutenant L. Brown and Leading Airman Hollowood—were shot down by the close-range automatic flak, apparently at their torpedo release points. Several other aircraft of the second wave were slightly damaged, but reached *Victorious* and landed at about 1100, preceded by the first wave and followed by all of the shadowers.

This was the Royal Navy's torpedo-bombers' only chance to cripple *Tirpitz* on the high seas. The Captain of *Victorious*, H. C. Bovell, RN, blamed the strike leader, who had initiated the attack too early, with his supporting sub-flights in unfavourable positions. Lieutenant P. G. Sugden, DSC, RN, had led the second wave to a good position and had come very close to scoring a hit. Had all twelve Albacores been thus co-ordinated, the outcome might have been different. The excessive release ranges cannot be blamed entirely on the aircrew: the assessment of range of fast ships can only be made with experience, and for several months the Home Fleet had not made capital ships available

for the express purpose of training the torpedo-bomber squadrons.

Having provided live torpedo practice for *Victorious*' squadrons, *Tirpitz* and *Friedrich Ihn* reached Narvik during the afternoon of 9 March. If Admiral Tovey and Captain Bovell were not impressed with the strike, the same cannot be said of the command aboard *Tirpitz*. So far as they were concerned, they had been attacked by 25 Swordfish, each of which had released two torpedoes. Some had even closed to 220 yards(200m) to release. The flak batteries had fired 345 rounds of 105mm(4.1in) and 4,269 rounds of 37mm and 20mm, and the secondary battery had added a dozen rounds, while the main 15in(380mm) battery had fired two full broadsides in a controlled barrage, and two rounds in long-range barrage. Three Swordfish were claimed shot down and many others damaged.

Tirpitz had escaped unscathed, but the experience left a scar on the German High Command. Grand Admiral Raeder questioned the validity of the original strategy behind the sortie, which had sunk only one empty straggler. But Hitler took a more positive line, insisting that *Tirpitz* should not be used in this fashion again if the positions of the Home Fleet aircraft carriers were not known precisely. The battleship was a deterrent against British invasion in the North, and was to be preserved as such—no raiding operation would justify her loss.

Two points of maritime strategy did not escape Hitler's notice—the offensive threat posed by the aircraft carrier, and the unhindered arrival of PQ12 in North Russian ports. To balance Britain's advantage in the former, he gave orders that the incomplete carrier *Graf Zeppelin* be taken in hand for completion, and that the unfinished heavy cruiser *Seydlitz* and the liner *Potsdam* should be converted as carriers. The *Graf Zeppelin* programme had ground to a halt in 1940, thanks in large measure to the jealousy of the Luftwaffe. This same 'war within a war'—common experience to all navies competing with independent air forces—was a contributory factor in the failure of this renewed plan for a German carrier fleet.

The matter of the passage of the PQ convoys, influencing, as they did, the progress of the war on the Eastern Front, was taken in hand immediately. The Luftwaffe in Northern Norway was reinforced by the arrival of two recently-trained torpedo-bomber Geschwader (KG26 and KG30) and a Gruppe of Fw 200C long-range reconnaissance aircraft (I/KG40). The latter had to be transferred from Bordeaux to Trondheim and thus the German offensive reconnaissance force in the Atlantic was weakened. U-boats were also moved to Norway: at one time, Hitler stated that he wanted all operational boats in this area, but this was later amended and the 'official' total reduced to 20 per cent of all boats.

Tirpitz left Narvik late on 12 March and reached Trondheim on the following evening. Four Allied submarines had been given patrol areas along the route, and seven Home Fleet destroyers searched off Horten Light in the early hours of 13 March, all without success in the prevailing bad weather.

After *Tirpitz* had refuelled on return to Trondheim, it was realised that she and her destroyers had consumed 8,100 tons of fuel oil in this one brief sortie, depleting stocks at Tromsö and Trondheim. The German merchant and naval services were not well provided with large tankers, and the maintenance of stocks of fuel for the growing number of large warships in Norway became a major problem. *Tirpitz* alone was using nearly 1,200 tons per month just sitting in a fiord and conducting occasional weapons practices, topping up from the naval tanker *Nordmark*, which, in turn, had to be replenished by tankers threatened by submarine and air attack themselves.

So far, *Tirpitz* had enjoyed almost complete peace in her anchorages. Lying close in to steep cliffs and hemmed in by booms and anti-torpedo netting, she was a difficult target even without the vagaries of the Norwegian weather to obscure her. An RAF Bomber Command attack by seven Short Stirlings of No 15 Squadron and nine Handley Page Halifaxes of No 76 Squadron on the night of 30/31 January 1942 had been rendered totally abortive by the weather, and two months later, an attack by 34 Halifaxes was foiled by an extensive smokescreen. One Halifax, of No 76 Squadron, bombed *Tirpitz*, but the 4,000lb(1,818kg) Medium Capacity bomb and four 500lb(227kg) General Purpose bombs fell some distance from the ship. Six Halifaxes failed to return.

This attack, on 30/31 March 1942, was intended to be part of the protective arrangements for convoy PQ13, which lost two ships to aircraft, two to U-boats, and one to destroyers. Only one ship was lost from PQ14, in mid April, and she was a U-boat victim; at the same time, QP10 lost four ships to aircraft and U-boats. When PQ15 and QP11 sailed at the end of April, their passage escort was strengthened, and the RAF was asked to make an offensive contribution.

At this time, Bomber Command was very restricted by its range of bombs, which were intended primarily for attacks on buildings. The 500/250lb(226.8/113.4kg) Semi-Armour-Piercing weapons used for shipping strikes by Coastal Command were too light for *Tirpitz*, and the 4,000lb(1,814.4kg) 'blockbuster' was just that— a light case blast bomb with no penetrative qualities: it would explode on impact with water, so that there would be no mining effect from near-misses. As warships can only be sunk by the ingress of water, it was necessary that some form of underwater weapon be improvised. In March, the RAF obtained about 100 Mark XIX anti-submarine mines from the Royal Navy, and strengthened them for release from aircraft, removing the sinker and mooring mechanism and installing a hydrostatic firing pistol which would detonate the 100lb(45.45kg) charge of Minol at 30 feet(9m) underwater. Although the mine now weighed 1,000lb(454.5kg), neither the size of the charge nor its firing depth was great enough to inflict major damage.

Tirpitz was still moored close inshore at Foettenfjord when 26 Halifaxes of Bomber Command's No 4 Group and 10 Lancasters of No 5 Group attacked in two waves on the clear moonlit night of 27/28 April. The first wave, at 4,000 to 6,000 feet(1,200 to 1,800m), released 4,000lb(1,814.4kg), 500lb(226.8kg) and 250lb (113.4kg) bombs, claiming several near-misses, while the second wave, of 11 Halifaxes of No 76 Squadron, dropped four Mk XIXN mines apiece, from low altitude. None exploded sufficiently close to cause any damage to *Tirpitz*, for the bombers' approach had been seriously hampered by a dense smoke screen, making target location extremely difficult. Other targets in the Trondheim area were bombed by aircraft unable to find *Tirpitz*, and four Halifaxes and a Lancaster failed to return.

On the following night, 23 Halifaxes and 11 Lancasters set out to repeat the attack. Of these, 30 attacked *Tirpitz* and one attacked *Prinz Eugen* and *Scheer*. Again no damage was inflicted on the battleship, although one Halifax claimed to have straddled her with mines. In addition to the *Tirpitz* attack force, Bomber Command had despatched an anti-flak force of 10 Lancasters and 9 Halifaxes, and thanks to their attentions, only two aircraft failed to return.

The Germans were unimpressed by the conventional bombing, but the use of the mines gave them pause. The discovery of several weapons on the steep slopes above the fiord, and in the shallows inshore, led them to believe that the mines were intentionally dropped so as to roll down into deeper water under *Tirpitz*. In fact, no such devious plan had been intended, but henceforward, *Tirpitz*'s anchorages were provided with sea-bed nets to arrest the travel of rolling charges dropped on adjacent shallows or land.

4

Operation 'Rösselsprung'

No plans were made for *Tirpitz* to interfere with PQ16/QP12 during the latter part of May 1942, and although *Scheer* and *Lützow* were both readied for a sortie from Narvik, the Luftwaffe was unable to provide the absolutely gap-free reconnaissance needed to locate the Home Fleet, as demanded by Hitler. German air anti-shipping strikes were, however, on the heaviest scale so far, although only six ships were sunk and three damaged by the approximately 200 dive- and torpedo-bomber sorties. U-boats were responsible for a seventh casualty in PQ16 and all three in QP12.

By mid-June 1942, sufficient fuel oil had been accumulated in north Norway for the SKL to approve (in principle) a major Fleet operation against the next PQ convoy. By now, the German naval concentration in Norway was impressive—*Tirpitz*, two pocket battleships, a heavy cruiser, a light cruiser, and ten large destroyers—particularly if it could be used in combination with the Luftwaffe's 160 anti-shipping strike and 74 long-range reconnaissance aircraft based around the North Cape. Unfortunately for the Germans, Luftflotte 5's success against PQ16 had been grossly overestimated—to the extent that it was believed that the entire 35-ship convoy had been destroyed after dispersal during the first day's attacks. Such an erroneous assessment ought to have been an indication of the inexperience of the strike and shadowing crews, but it was taken at face value by the Luftwaffe's commanders, who saw no urgent need for close co-operation with the navy.

The Admiralty, however, credited the Germans with a higher degree of inter-service co-operation and, with clear evidence that aircraft could track the convoys almost continuously, grew increasingly nervous about the possibilities of a co-ordinated onslaught. This nervousness was not shared to the same extent by the British and American ships of the Home Fleet, nor by the operational commanders, who wished to bring the German Fleet to action.

PQ17 sailed from Reykjavik on 27 June 1942, and was sighted by U-boats and reconnaissance aircraft on 1 July. QP13 had been sighted on the previous day, but this convoy was to be left to the Luftwaffe, while the warships attacked the more important eastbound convoy. Operation 'Rösselsprung' ('Knight's Move') began on 2 July, when the SKL gave Vice-Admiral Schniewind, now Flag Officer Battleships, permission to position the ships for the sortie. Hitler had given permission for the operation, with the proviso that the Home Fleet carrier must be found before the German Fleet left harbour for the attack on the convoy. *Lützow*, *Scheer* and six destroyers left Narvik for Altenfjord, while *Tirpitz*, *Hipper* and four destroyers left Trondheim for an anchorage in the Lofoten Islands—all undetected by British air reconnaissance, which was incomplete due to cloud in the two base areas. The preliminary movement was not without casualties: *Lützow* ran aground while leaving Ofotfjord on 2 July, and three of *Tirpitz*'s destroyers grounded on arrival in Gimsöystraumen on 3 July, leaving only the faithful *Friedrich Ihn*, joined later by *Richard Beitzen*.

In the afternoon of 3 July, air reconnaissance disclosed that *Tirpitz* and *Hipper* had left Trondheim, but continued bad weather in the Narvik/Lofotens area prevented their re-location or the discovery that *Scheer* and six destroyers were loose. Even if the air reconnaissances were to continue to fail, there was still a triple barrier of 13 British, Russian and French submarines between north Norway and the convoy route.

During the night of 3/4 July, the *Tirpitz* group left for Altenfjord to join *Scheer*, once again undetected. PQ17 passed 40 miles to the north of Bear Island during the night, shadowed throughout by aircraft and U-boats. The Germans were also aware that the Home Fleet, with *Duke of York*, *Washington*, *Victorious* and two cruisers, was between Jan Mayen Land and Bear Island. Admiral Tovey's intentions were to cover PQ17 from a position 200 miles to the north-west of Bear Island, so that *Victorious*' Albacores could be on hand should the German surface threat materialise.

The first major Luftwaffe attacks were delivered on 4 July, three ships being sunk and another damaged by torpedoes. In the late evening, when the last attack had been driven off, PQ17 was 300 miles north of the North Cape, still in good order with only 900 miles to run to Archangel. Two British and two American heavy cruisers and three destroyers were still within sight, although they were to withdraw to the west during the night. The submarine barrier was being re-positioned to new lines north-east of North Cape, but there were no reports from the Russian submarines guarding the approaches to Tromsö and Altenfjord. Six Consolidated PBY-5 Catalinas of Nos 210 and 240 Squadrons RAF had begun operations from Lake Lakhta, near Archangel, on 4 July, flying cross-over patrols across the route from North Cape to PQ17's track, but their searches had proved negative. The only positive information was that *Scheer* had left Narvik—a discovery made 48 hours after the event.

A thousand miles away, in London, the First Sea Lord, Admiral Sir Dudley Pound, called a Naval Staff meeting. He had no positive information as to the position of the German ships, merely negative reports —*Tirpitz* and the pocket battleships were not in their usual anchorages. Far removed from the scene of potential action, he did not see fit to formulate an appraisal for the C-in-C Home Fleet, upon which the latter could act at discretion, but chose to take temporary control of a situation which existed mainly in his own apprehension.

On the assumption that a German surface force could engage the convoy, destroying it and its cruiser close cover at any time after 0200 on 5 July, Pound signalled to the cruiser force commander that the cruisers were to withdraw at high speed (signal timed 2111/4th), and that the convoy was to 'disperse' and continue independently to Russian ports. This meant that the ships would no longer remain in convoy formation, but would follow much the same routes to the same destinations, at their individual convenient speeds. Although this was far inferior to convoy for defensive purposes, the ships would remain close together for several hours, and the route could be patrolled by escorts. But Admiral Pound did not mean the convoy to disperse, which still left it very vulnerable to attack by heavy warships, and at 2136 he gave the order to 'scatter', which meant that the ships would leave the convoy on divergent tracks. Scattering would reduce losses to surface ships, which could not spare the time to round up the victims, but it also made protection impossible. PQ17 duly scattered at 2215 on 4 July, 800 miles from Archangel and 360 miles from Altenfjord, where *Tirpitz* still lay, having achieved her most significant success simply by changing anchorages.

On 5 July, six merchant ships were sunk by bombs, and six by U-boats. Hitler finally agreed to allow 'Rösselsprung' to proceed during the forenoon, after learning of the position of the Home Fleet, which was some 190 miles north-west of Bear Island. The German fleet was ordered to leave Altenfjord at 1137 and actually got under way in the early afternoon. As soon as *Tirpitz*, *Scheer*, and *Hipper* reached the open sea, the efficiency of the Allied close-reconnaissance screen was demonstrated. At 1700, a Russian submarine sighted and attacked *Tirpitz* 45 miles north-west of the North Cape. Two torpedo hits were claimed by *K.21*, but none was scored, and the Germans were unaware of the attack. At 1816, an hour after *K.21* reported the sighting, a Catalina from Grasnaya, near Archangel, sighted and reported *Tirpitz* to the north-east of the North Cape, and finally the British submarine *P.54* (later renamed *Unshaken*) sighted smoke and aircraft at 1929, and an hour later reported *Tirpitz* and *Hipper* and six destroyers to be 55 miles east-north-east of the North Cape. Attempting to close on the surface, *P.54* was driven down by aircraft and could not get within 10 miles of the enemy, but her reports were of considerable value.

The German monitoring service had intercepted the sightings, and the SKL calculated that, armed with these reports, the Home Fleet and its aircraft carrier could close the North Cape sufficiently to be able to intercept the returning ships if the operation continued. The capacity of *Luftflotte 5* to intervene decisively was apparently ignored—it was better that the Ju 88s and He 111s should deal with the scattered convoy and that the fleet should not run any risk at all. At 2132, Admiral Schniewind was ordered to abandon 'Rösselsprung' and return to Altenfjord. This order was obeyed, and the German fleet subsequently proceeded to Bogenfjord, Narvik, on 7 July, being sighted on passage by an RAF Catalina from Vaenga (Murmansk).

PQ17 had lost 15 ships by the close of 5 July. By 28 July, when the last of 11 survivors arrived at Molotovsk, another four merchant ships and a naval tanker had been sunk by bombs and four ships had been sunk by U-boats. Two ships had returned safely to Iceland. The Luftwaffe claimed full responsibility for the victory, believing that the last torpedo attack on 4 July had led to the scattering, but the aircraft were only the agents of a victory which had been 'set up' for them by the mere threat of intervention by *Tirpitz*.

5

The Latent Threat

The next eastbound convoy operation was to have commenced on 16 July 1942, and *Tirpitz* was brought to readiness from 18 to 21 of that month. There was a similar alert between 7 and 15 August, but PQ18 had been delayed owing to the need to detach considerable strength from the Home Fleet to fight a convoy through to Malta in mid August. *Tirpitz* had now been out of dock for over a year, and, lacking the necessary maintenance facilities, her list of defects was becoming embarrassingly long—gun mountings and fire-control systems, boilers and main turbines, and various electrical installations all required attention if she were to remain a fully battleworthy unit. In spite of the recommendations of Captain E. Topp, her captain, Hitler would not countenance *Tirpitz*'s return to Germany for repairs, believing that an Allied landing in Norway was still probable.

While these signals were being exchanged between Norway and Germany, in the opening days of September 1942, PQ18 was leaving Iceland for Russia. The convoy's close escort was stronger, and included an escort carrier—*Avenger*—primarily for fighter defence, but although there were two battleships with the Home Fleet cover, no Fleet carrier was available. To make up for this deficiency in the torpedo striking force, 32 Handley Page Hampden torpedo-bombers of No 144 Squadron RAF and No 455 Squadron Royal Australian Air Force flew to Vaenga, near Murmansk, 23 actually arriving on 4 September. Long-range maritime patrol reinforcement for the Russian area commander was provided by 14 Catalinas of No 210 Squadron RAF and 422 Squadron RCAF, while four photographic-reconnaissance Spitfires Mark VII of No 541 Squadron would watch Narvik for signs of movement by the German ships.

In the event, the German ships detailed for the attack on PQ18 proceeded only from Bogenfjord to Altenfjord, reported en route by the four Allied submarines positioned to look out for them. *Tirpitz* was not to be included in the force even if considered fit for action, at Hitler's express order, and the remainder were not allowed to sail because Admiral Raeder considered the risks too great.

PQ18 was attacked by aircraft and U-boats between the morning of 13 and afternoon of 15 September, and again in the forenoon of 18 September. Ten ships were sunk by torpedo-bombers and three by U-boats, but at a cost of 33 out of the 92 torpedo-bombers in Norway, eight other aircraft, and three U-boats. U-boats also sank six ships out of QP14, returning as PQ18 went out. Thus 16 out of 54 merchant ships in convoy (the other three ships were naval) were lost in the last major air offensive against a North Russian convoy. The safe arrival of 26 freighters in Russia demonstrated that the Royal Navy would not yield again to a mere threat.

There were no more eastbound convoys until mid December 1942, due to the build-up for, and execution of, the Anglo-American landings in North Africa in November. On 23 October, *Tirpitz* left Bogenfjord and returned to Foettenfjord, Trondheim, for a refit. Repairs and overhaul were undertaken in stages, so that the ship was never completely immobilised, but a surprising amount of necessary work was carried out, considering the primitive conditions and distance from her sources of supply and skilled labour.

During this period, a most enterprising attack was attempted on *Tirpitz* by a combined Norwegian/Royal Navy team, using a 'requisitioned' fishing boat, *Arthur*, to carry a pair of two-man human torpedoes ('Chariots') to the Norwegian coast from the Shetlands. On arrival in the approaches to Trondheim on 30 October, the Chariots were lowered into the water and towed under *Arthur*, whose Norwegian skipper, Leif Larsen, bluffed his way past the German guard-boats with the aid of forged permits and licences. By the early hours of 31 October, *Arthur* was past all the check points and only four and a half miles from *Tirpitz*, when the Chariots broke away and sank as the little drifter plunged into a choppy sea. The four Norwegians and six Britons scuttled *Arthur* and made off over the mountains to Sweden. In a skirmish with guards near the border, one of the British ratings was wounded and captured. Under interrogation by the Gestapo he admitted that he had been one of a party of under-water saboteurs; following a directive from Hitler that all 'commandos' taken in Norway were not to be accorded the normal status of prisoners of war, the rating was executed in January 1943.

The news of the attempt came as a complete surprise to the German Navy. Measures were taken to protect *Tirpitz* within the net defences, by means of more efficient hydrophone watchkeeping and by equipping the guard-boats with depth-charges. The surveillance and control of local craft was also made more stringent, although in view of the importance of Trondheim as a centre of Norwegian commerce and administration, the increased load on the control service absorbed more naval manpower. While complaining of the general lack of fixed defences, the local naval authorities also pointed out that, as of the beginning of December 1942, there were only 14 serviceable Bf 109F fighters (of the IVth Gruppe of Jagdgeschwader 5) to defend the Trondheim area, and the German Navy's most important ship. There were, however, no immediate plans for an air attack by the RAF, Bomber Command being more pre-occupied with area attacks on German cities and industry.

By 28 December, *Tirpitz* was ready for sea trials after her refit. It was not the most auspicious time to return to service, for the last day of 1942 was one of the unhappiest of the entire war for the German Navy. The first of the new 'season' of eastbound convoys—redesignated JW for security reasons—was divided into two parts, JW51A and JW51B, and sailed on 15 and 22 December, respectively. JW51A went completely undetected by the Germans, but JW51B was reported by a U-boat south of Bear Island on 30 December. Vice-Admiral O. Kummetz sailed at once from Alten-fjord to intercept with a force consisting of *Lützow*, *Hipper* and six destroyers. JW51B's escort amounted to five smaller destroyers, two corvettes, and an armed trawler, with a minesweeper near by, and two light cruisers within 50 miles. Action was joined shortly before dawn on 31 December, 220 miles to the north-west of Murmansk, and ended four hours later. The convoy was unharmed, the escort had suffered the loss of a destroyer and the minesweeper, and another destroyer was severely damaged. The attack on the convoy had not been pressed home and Kummetz's force lost a destroyer; his flagship, *Hipper*, was set on fire and damaged sufficiently seriously to require her return to Germany for repairs. Undoubtedly, Hitler's circumscribing orders on the employment of heavy

ships had hindered Admiral Kummetz, but the latter had possessed an overwhelming local superiority which had been set at nought by the high morale and initiative of the weak escort.

The full enormity of the failure was not generally realised for several days, due to 'communications "problems"', but as early as 1 January 1943, Hitler informed Raeder that he intended to decommission the cruisers and capital ships of the German fleet. On 6 January, he summoned the naval C-in-C to the OKW headquarters and harangued him for over an hour on the historical insignificance of the part played by German major warships in the two World Wars, summing up by stating that the fleet's crews would be better employed in the U-boat Fleet, and the guns in shore emplacements. Raeder offered to resign and Hitler did not decline the offer. On 14 January, Raeder forwarded a memorandum to Hitler, explaining current naval strategy—the 'Fleet in Being' principle, which proposed that a powerful, intact fleet did not have to leave harbour to tie down stronger Allied forces, preventing them from being deployed in more active theatres of war, such as the Indian Ocean or Pacific.

Such a negative strategy had no appeal for Hitler. He ordered Raeder to suspend all construction and large repairs, and to recall all ships of above destroyer size to Germany for decommissioning. Admiral Karl Doenitz, the Flag-Officer U-boats, relieved Raeder on 30 January, and on 8 February he submitted his scheme for the run-down of the fleet to Hitler. In the course of the next three weeks, however, Doenitz's eyes were opened to the wider implications of a balanced maritime strategy, and by 26 February, he was facing in the opposite direction, submitting another scheme, this time for the fuller employment of the fleet against the Russian convoys, and the transfer of *Scharnhorst* to Norway. At first unenthusiastic, Hitler was eventually swayed by Doenitz's advocacy.

Tirpitz returned to full operational status on 24 January 1943, and resumed exercises in the Trondheim area, working up after the refit period. The work-up lasted until 5 March, when she was put under orders to sail to Bogenfjord, Narvik, to join *Scharnhorst* and *Lützow*. Sailing on 11 March, she arrived on the night of 12/13 March, having made an undetected passage. A few days later, the Narvik force put to sea to exercise, proceeding afterwards to Altenfjord to await the movement of convoy JW54. New orders issued by the SKL and approved by Doenitz had given priority to the destruction of convoys over the absolute preservation of the fleet for anti-invasion duties, and it was hoped that great success would attend future raiding operations by the 'First Task Force'.

The hopes were not realised. Aware that the Germans had achieved their maximum possible concentration in north Norway, the C-in-C Home Fleet, Admiral Sir Bruce Fraser, submitted that the sailing of North Russian convoys should be suspended. At the same time, the U-boats were enjoying the last of their successful phases in the North Atlantic and the Admiralty withdrew the Home Fleet escorts to reinforce the Atlantic convoy defences. JW54A and B did not leave the United Kingdom until mid-November 1943—the German Fleet was thus left 'all dressed-up with nowhere to go', exercising, conducting gunnery training, and wondering how to maintain morale so far from home with so little to do.

At last, on 6 September 1943, an operational task was found for *Tirpitz* and *Scharnhorst*. On 8 September, with a screen of ten destroyers, they sailed to bombard the Anglo-Norwegian weather reporting station on Spitzbergen—Operation 'Sizilien/Zitronella'. The station was able to send a distress signal before it was silenced, but it took the ships of the First Task Force nearly six hours to complete the task of wrecking the virtually undefended base. *Tirpitz* fired 52 rounds of 380mm(15in) and 82 rounds of 150mm (5.9in)—the only combat use of her low-angle armament against surface targets. The Home Fleet had sailed on 7 September, after an aircraft reconnaissance had reported the absence of the two big ships from Altenfjord, but the German ships returned to their base without interference on 9 September.

6
Operation 'Source'

The Spitzbergen sortie caused considerable alarm in the Admiralty. There were no obvious targets for the German force, but long-laid plans for an attack on the ships would be upset if the absence from Altenfjord were prolonged.

In 1941, the Admiralty had ordered the construction of two prototype midget submarines, X-3 and X-4, for use as minelayers in coastal waters. X-3 began trials early in 1942, and the suitability of this type of 51ft(15.54m)-long, 27 ton submerged displacement craft for attacks on sheltered anchorages was quickly appreciated. In May 1942, Vickers-Armstrongs Ltd were given a contract for the construction of six 'production' midget submarines—X-5 to X-10. All were to be fitted to carry 'side charges', two-ton containers filled with Amatex high-explosives, and shaped to conform to the sides of the hull of the X-craft. The midget submarine would close the anchored enemy, release the side charges below, and then evacuate the area before the charges detonated, triggered by a mechanical clock device.

The operational X-craft were all delivered by mid January 1943, and it was hoped to send them out to attack Tirpitz at Trondheim before 9 March; after that date, daylight would be too long for assured success. It was soon apparent that the crews of the X-craft could not be worked-up in time, and the operation was postponed until mid September, when the nights would be sufficiently long.

The delay was undoubtedly beneficial. Not only were the crews given a more relaxed training schedule, but the administrative and support facilities were more comprehensive than they might otherwise have been. On 17 April 1943, the 12th Submarine Flotilla was formed, with a specially adapted depot ship—Bonaventure—which could hoist X-craft inboard for workshop repairs, fitting of charges, and straightforward routine cleaning and maintenance. Bonaventure and her Flotilla moved to Loch Cairnbawn, in the remote north-west corner of Scotland, in June, and in

July the X-craft were provided with Home Fleet capital ships as targets, to practise approaches and laying the charges. By 1 September 1943, all training and preparations were complete, and six patrol submarines had arrived at Loch Cairnbawn to practise towing the X-craft and transferring personnel under way. (The tow ropes used for the operation were of nylon—an early use of the material for this purpose.)

Up-to-date information of the position of the ships in Altenfjord was an urgent need; as the mobility of the midget submarines was severely limited by their 2-knots submerged speed, knowledge of the targets' whereabouts had to be exact. On 3 September, therefore, three Spitfire PR VII high-altitude reconnaissance aircraft of No 541 Squadron RAF were despatched from Leuchars, Fife, to Vaenga to fly twice-daily sorties over Altenfjord, and on the next day, Mosquitoes of No 540 Squadron began shuttle trips between Leuchars and Vaenga, taking photographs of all the anchorages in northern Norway on both the outward and inward trips. With such over-target frequency, it was not surprising that the disappearance of the German fleet on 6 September was noted immediately, to the understandable consternation of the Admiralty and the 10th Flotilla. It was with considerable relief that the return to Altenfjord on 9 September was promptly noted by the reconnaissance detachment.

The first five X-craft left Loch Cairnbawn during the afternoon of 11 September. Thrasher, Truculent and Stubborn towing X-5, X-6, and X-7, which were to attack Tirpitz at Kaafjord, and Sea Nymph and Syrtis with X-8 and X-9 to attack Lützow and Scharnhorst, respectively, in Langefjord. Sceptre, towing X-10, also to attack Scharnhorst, had less distance to run to her release sector off Söröy Island, and did not leave harbour until the next day. The weather remained fair until midnight 14/15 September, the 'parent' submarines running on the surface while the X-craft remained submerged, surfacing only to renew the air in the boats every four hours. In the early hours of 15

September, X-8 broke loose from *Sea Nymph* without the latter being aware of the parting of the tow; the stray midget met up with *Stubborn* and *X-7*, who had also experienced a broken tow, wandered off again in the early hours of 16 September, and was eventually taken in tow once again by *Sea Nymph* late that afternoon, after forty hours of uncomfortable independence. At about the time that *X-8* inadvertently parted company with *Stubborn*, *X-9* dived after ventilating and was not seen again by *Syrtis*, which searched for 36 hours after realising that the tow had parted.

X-8's troubles were not yet over. During the afternoon of 17 September, it was discovered that her side charges were leaking and both were jettisoned, one exploding at 1,000 yards(900m) and causing no embarrassment to *X-8* or *Sea Nymph*, and the other exploding at 7,000 yards(6,400m) and crippling *X-8* so that she had to be scuttled, while *Sea Nymph* suffered from a number of broken gauge glasses.

Thrasher, *Truculent*, and *Sceptre* and their X-craft enjoyed uneventful passages to the release area, the first two arriving on 17 September, *Sceptre* on 19th, and *Stubborn* on 20 September. The crews who were to make the attacks were transferred to the midgets, and the long-suffering 'passage crews' moved to the relative roominess of the patrol submarines, which released the X-craft in the approaches to Altenfjord during the early evening of 20 September. It had previously been agreed between the X-craft captains that charges should be laid between 0500 and 0800 on 22 September, and that no one should attempt to penetrate the net defences before 0100 on 22 September.

X-5, *X-6*, *X-7* and *X10* passed the first line of defence—a minefield off Söröy Island—during the night of 20/21 September, and the single auxiliary patrol vessel in Stjernsund during 21 September. *X-5* had not been seen since the previous evening and, of the others, only *X-7* had been free of material defects, *X-6* having developed a periscope problem and *X-10* a multiplicity of defects. Nevertheless, all were within striking distance of *Tirpitz* and *Scharnhorst* by the evening of 21 September, when they stopped to charge batteries and ventilate. All that lay between them and their targets were the net defences.

In *Tirpitz*'s anchorage, the net defences stretched from shore to shore across the mouth of Kaafjord, enclosing a number of berths, each with its own separate netting. The Kaafjord net—155ft(47.25m) deep—was passed without difficulty, the X-craft using the 440yard(400m) 'gate' where the netting was only 33ft(10m) deep. The enclosure at Barbrudalen,

where *Tirpitz* was lying, was protected by a 50ft(15.24m) double anti-torpedo net, below which a net of looser mesh stretched down to the sea bed. The only access to Barbrudalen was through a 66ft(20m)-wide gate, where the net had a maximum depth of 110ft(33.5m). On the night before the attack, this net was left open: the ship-shore telephone had broken down and there was continuous boat traffic between the ship and the shore headquarters at Bossekop. Aware of the opportunities which this offered to an underwater enemy, *Tirpitz*'s captain ordered that a continuous hydrophone watch be maintained by the ship until 0600 on 22 September.

In the event, neither the gap nor the precautions benefitted the battleship or the approaching X-craft, except possibly *X-5*. *X-6*, commanded by Lieutenant D. Cameron, RNR, ran through the open gate at 0705 and, suffering from a flooded periscope, grounded and was sighted on the battleship's port beam. Thereafter, *X-6* was seriously hampered by the lack of a periscope and the failure of the gyro compass. Cameron pin-pointed his target by her shadow, and pressed in to release his charges abreast *Tirpitz*'s 'B' turret. *X-6* was scuttled under fire, and the four-man crew taken off by a motor boat from the battleship.

X-7 had previously become involved in a net enclosure, formerly occupied by *Lützow*, and had spent an hour getting out again before Lieutenant B.C.G. Place, DSC, RN, succeeded in wriggling through the Barbrudalen nets, at about 0715. Place sighted *Tirpitz* less than 50 yards(46m) away, coming to the surface after passing the net, and he laid his charges deliberately, one under 'B' turret, near Cameron's two charges, and the other between the centre engine room and 'C' turret. The next 15 minutes were taken up in getting out of the nets again, this time over the top and under fire from *Tirpitz*'s close-range AA guns. By now, *X-7* was difficult to control and the gyro compass was not functioning, and Place's attempts to clear the area before the charges exploded were unsuccessful.

Lieutenant Cameron and his crew were, by now, aboard *Tirpitz*, and the battleship's personnel were aware that some underwater device was in the vicinity of the ship, either attached to the hull, or lying on the sea bed, 115 to 130ft(35 to 40m) below the keel. There was some indecision as to the best way to avoid damage, but as unknown dangers might have been lurking outside Barbrudalen, it was positively decided not to leave the protection of the nets. A wire was dragged along the bottom and sides of the ship, from bow to stern, to dislodge any charges attached to the hull, and the bows were swung to starboard, by heaving in on the starboard mooring cable and veering the port cable, to bring the ship away from the position where *X-6* had sunk. A motor boat, armed with hand grenades, had been running around the enclosure since approximately 0715, but apart from this patrol, and opening fire on any suspicious object in the vicinity, there was little further to be done by *Tirpitz*, except to ensure that all watertight doors were shut.

Lieutenant Place's second charge exploded about 20ft(6m) from the port side, abreast the centre engine room, at 0812, followed almost immediately by another charge 200ft(61m) off the port bow. *Tirpitz* whipped violently, injuring 65 men, and most of the lighting circuits and nearly all electrical systems failed. Flooding was limited to empty protective spaces outboard on the port side near the explosion aft, to No 2 Diesel Generator Room, some double-bottom compartments, and a number of port-side wing fuel tanks. The immediate list of 1° was corrected by counter-flooding in the port and centre engine rooms, the flak-control transmitting station, and No 1 DG Room. The bed plates of most of the diesel generators were cracked and, for a time, only one DG was available to supply all the ship's electrical needs.

At the moment that the charges went off, *X-7* was barely 110 yards(100m) distant, having blundered into the anti-torpedo netting from the outside. The shock freed the midget, but put all the remaining instruments out of action making her virtually impossible to control, so that although Lieutenant Place continued to attempt to escape, *X-7* broke surface several times, being exposed to fire on each occasion. At 0835, finding himself close to a target buoy 220 yards(200m) off *Tirpitz*'s starboard bow, Lieutenant Place deliberately surfaced in order to evacuate his crew. However, as he stepped on to the buoy, *X-7* sank, taking with her the three remaining members of the crew. Only one, Sub-Lieutenant R. Aitken, RNVR, managed to escape, using the Davis Submarine Escape Apparatus to surface at 1115.

Meanwhile, at 0843, a third midget submarine broke surface 350 yards(320m) off the battleship's starboard beam, and was immediately taken under fire by the close-range and 105mm(4.1in) flak; hit repeatedly, the submarine sank, and the position was thoroughly depth-charged by the destroyer *Z-27*. The last midget was presumably *X-5*, commanded by Lieutenant H. Henty-Creer, RNVR. Last sighted by *X-6* and *X-7* off Söröy before midnight on 20 September, nothing is known of her subsequent movements, and it is possible that Lieutenant Henty-Creer had actually penetrated and escaped from Barbrudalen undetected, and then suffered shock effects similar to *X-7*.

For their successful attack on *Tirpitz*, Lieutenants Cameron and Place were awarded the Victoria Cross, and all surviving members of their crews were decorated. *X-10*, which was to have attacked *Scharnhorst*, suffered from a plague of defects: gyro compass failure and a fire in the periscope hoist motor led Lieutenant K.R. Hudspeth, RANVR, to abandon the attempt (when within five miles of Kaafjord) and he jettisoned his charges 12 hours after he had felt eleven heavy explosions at the time of the intended attack. Returning to the pre-agreed rendezvous area, *X-10* waited 50 hours off Söröy before making contact with *Stubborn* shortly after midnight on 27/28 September. The return passage was made difficult by heavy seas, and *X-10* eventually had to be abandoned on the evening of 3 October.

Stock-taking aboard *Tirpitz*, during the forenoon of 22 September, revealed that, although her watertight integrity was but little affected, there was much damage to the propulsion machinery and the gunnery fire-control systems. All turbine feet, propeller shaft plummer and thrust blocks and auxiliary machinery bearers were cracked or distorted, and the port turbine casing and condenser casing were fractured. The propellers could not be turned and the port rudder unit was out of action due to flooding of the steering-gear compartment through a gland damaged by the whip of the ship.

All the main armament turrets jumped off their roller paths—the turntables which took the entire weight of the turrets, but only 'A' and 'C' turrets, closest to the explosions, were out of action for more than a few hours; the after port side 5.8in(150mm) turret (P.III) was, however, completely jammed. The main armament director control towers were undamaged, but the only optical range-finders left serviceable were those on the foretop and on 'B' turret: the conning-tower range-finder and that in 'D' turret were completely wrecked, while the secondary armament range-finders all needed replacement. Both of the after flak directors were damaged and out of action, and of the forward pair, only one was fully stabilised. Two Arado Ar196As, which had been on deck outside the hangars, were severely damaged, and the catapult was unserviceable. Of the personnel injured by concussion, one had died and 40 others required treatment.

It was clear that *Tirpitz* could not return to Germany for repairs without assistance and without risk from determined Allied air, surface and submarine attack. Air cover on the scale provided for the 'Channel Dash' in 1942 was simply not available in northern Norway, and the naval forces available for close escort were not sufficient defence against the Home Fleet. By 25

September, Hitler had agreed that *Tirpitz* would be repaired in Altenfjord. The work to be undertaken would have normally required the support of a fully equipped dockyard, and the attendance of representatives of the manufacturers of specialised technical equipment. No such facilities were available to *Tirpitz*: all replacement parts had to be brought from Germany by sea, and installed by the ship's staff with a minimum of outside assistance. Docking was out of the question (the German Navy possessed only one floating dock large enough for *Tirpitz*, and it is inconceivable that this dock could or would have been transferred to Norway) and divers repaired the splits in the hull with underwater cement; a coffer dam had to be constructed around the damaged port rudder in order to re-pack the glands.

Despite the difficulties, the bulk of the repair work was completed by the first week in March 1944—a remarkable achievement by any standards. *Tirpitz* left the Barbrudalen enclosure on 15 March, and on that day and the next, carried out 'harbour trials' of her main machinery and armament, all within the confines of Altenfjord. Defects, shown up by this brief run, were rectified during the succeeding two weeks and she was made ready for full power trials and de-gaussing calibration.

7

Operation 'Tungsten'

The Admiralty was aware of the progress of *Tirpitz*'s repairs, thanks to skilful interpretation and inference from the reconnaissance photographs, and also to reports from agents in Norway. Since 26 December 1943, when *Scharnhorst* had been sunk in action off the North Cape, there had been no major surface unit to threaten the JW/RA convoys and it had been possible to release Home Fleet ships for redeployment to the Far East or for refits. The German Navy had been effectively deterred from ever again attempting to intercept convoys with capital ships; indeed, the SKL was not yet certain as to the exact employment of *Tirpitz* when her repairs were complete, but as this was not known to the Admiralty, the latter decided to strike again, using carrier-borne aircraft.

By the beginning of 1944, the Royal Navy's air power was incomparably stronger than it had been in 1942. New carriers and aircraft had entered service during 1943, so that for Operation 'Tungsten', the planned attack on *Tirpitz*, there would be two fast fleet carriers (*Victorious* and *Furious*), three escort carriers armed with fighters (*Emperor*, *Pursuer* and *Searcher*), and one escort carrier (*Fencer*) to provide anti-submarine and fighter defence. Between them, these six ships carried 42 Fairey Barracudas, to be used as dive-bombers, 28 Vought F4U-1B Corsairs, 20 Grumman F6F-3 Hellcats and 40 Grumman FM-1 Wildcats, all to be used as escort fighters, and 14 Supermarine Seafires and eight Grumman F4F-4B Wildcats for fighter defence, with a dozen Fairey Swordfish A/S aircraft.

Planning for the operation began at the end of 1943, under the direction of Vice-Admiral Sir Henry Moore, the Second in Command, Home Fleet, and his Chief of Staff, Captain I. D. Mackintosh, who had previously commanded the carriers *Eagle* and *Victorious*. Variations in approach to the possible target areas were worked out, as were the air strike tactics and the 'weapons mix'. Reality for the training phase was achieved by the use of a full-scale practice range built at

Loch Eriboll. This included a buoyed area to represent *Tirpitz*, dummy flak batteries and smoke screen generators.

When planning began, *Victorious* was under refit, the two squadrons (829 and 831) of her No 52 Torpedo-Bomber-Reconnaissance Wing had not begun their combined work-up and, although one of her fighter squadrons (1834) arrived from the USA in December, the second (1836) did not reach this country until mid January 1944. Furthermore, the new bomb—the American 1,600lb(725.7kg) armour-piercing bomb—which, it was hoped, would inflict really serious damage on *Tirpitz*, was not cleared for release from the Barracuda until December 1943, and then only from specially strengthened aircraft.

Of the other carriers, only *Searcher* and *Emperor* had not seen previous action, although *Furious*' No 8 TBR Wing (827 and 830 Squadrons) was not 'blooded' until 11 February 1944.

'Tungsten' was originally planned to take place between 7 and 16 March, *before Tirpitz* would have completed repairs, but *Victorious*' refit was not completed in time and the operation was postponed by a fortnight. In fact, the delay was beneficial, for it permitted additional training for the TBR and Fighter Wings. This culminated in a full-scale dress rehearsal for the attack, on 28 March, using Loch Eriboll. *Furious* and *Victorious* exchanged 827 and 831 Squadrons in order that the two waves of the attack would each consist of a single TBR Wing, with *Victorious* launching 12 Barracudas each time and the smaller *Furious* flying off the other nine. The fighter support for each wave was to consist of a dozen Corsairs as medium-level top cover against interception, 10 Hellcats to strafe heavy flak batteries, and 20 Wildcats to attack *Tirpitz*'s automatic flak and directors—42 fighters accompanying each wave.

The 'Tungsten' force sailed in two parts. Force 1 left Scapa Flow during the forenoon of 30 March, and consisted of *Victorious*, *Duke of York*, *Anson*, a light cruiser and five destroyers, whose task until 1 April was to provide distant support for convoy JW58, which had left for Russia on 27 March. Force 2—*Furious, Searcher, Pursuer, Emperor, Fencer*, three light cruisers, two oilers, and five, later 10, destroyers—sailed later on 30 March, under the command of Rear-Admiral A. W. La Touche Bisset, Rear-Admiral, Escort Carriers. The two Forces were originally intended to rendezvous on 3 April, for a strike at dawn on the following day, but the good weather and the evident ability of JW58's escort, which included two escort carriers, to fend for the convoy unaided, induced the C-in-C Home Fleet, Admiral Sir Bruce Fraser, to advance the operation by 24 hours. At the same time, *Tirpitz*'s sea trials, scheduled for 1 April, were postponed for 48 hours as the result of an adverse weather forecast.

Forces 1 and 2 met during the afternoon of 2 April, some 250 miles to the north-west of Altenfjord. The C-in-C, in *Duke of York*, detached himself with two destroyers to a covering position to the north-west of Bear Island; the oilers and two destroyers proceeded to wait some 300 miles to the north-west of the North Cape, and Vice-Admiral Moore took the remainder of the fleet to the flying-off position, 120 miles north of Kaafjord, where the carriers arrived at 0415 on 3 April. Throughout the night, aircraft parked on the decks of the carriers were having their engines warmed through, and were then being exchanged with those which had enjoyed the warmth of the hangars throughout the chilly passage north. When the first strike wave started engines at 0405, there was not one failure to start, and all 61 aircraft took off safely.

The 21 Barracudas of No 8 TBR Wing, led by Lieutenant-Commander (A) R. Baker-Faulkner, RN, were carrying seven 1,600(725.7kg) AP bombs, twenty-four 500lb(226.8kg) semi-armour-piercing bombs to pierce the 2in(50mm) weather-deck armour, and twelve 500lb medium capacity and four 600lb (272.6kg) anti-submarine bombs for surface or underwater blast effect. Three 500lb bombs apiece were carried by 12 of the Barracudas, but only two 600lb A/s bombs could be carried by the remaining pair.

The strike formed up at low level, and took departure at 0437, remaining close to the sea to avoid premature detection by radar. Not until they were 25 miles from the Norwegian coast did the aircraft begin to climb to 10,000ft(3,000m), crossing the coast 37 miles north of *Tirpitz* at 0508. The German radar had detected '32-plus' aircraft three minutes earlier, but this alert did not reach the battleship's flak-control centre until four minutes before the attack began, at 0528. *Tirpitz* had already raised her port

anchor and cast off her stern lines, and the starboard anchor cable was 'straight up and down' when the first warning came. The main flak battery was already manned, but there was insufficient time for all damage-control precautions to be taken, so that 20 per cent of the watertight doors were still open.

The Barracudas, Hellcats and Wildcats deployed to attack from as many directions as possible, to divide the ship's defences; the Barracudas were, however, more limited than the fighters, for they had been briefed to attack along the line of the ship to obtain the maximum number of hits, and diving at between 40° and 70° from 8,000ft(2,438m), they were in sight throughout the run. The fighters followed the mountainous terrain, keeping *Tirpitz*'s 96ft(29.26m)-high foretop in sight until they came over the crests overlooking Kaafjord. While the 800 Squadron Hellcats attacked the heavy flak, 881 and 882 Squadrons' Wildcats put the ship's flak directors out of action, and inflicted serious personnel casualties on exposed guns' crews as well as damaging the gun mountings themselves with the armour-piercing 0.50in(12.7mm) rounds. Although the smoke-screen installations around the shores of the fiord had been started as the ship was being warned, the short notice did not permit the screen to develop sufficiently to distract either the fighters or the bombers.

The Barracudas were taken under fire at a range of some three miles, as they began their dive, but the 105mm(4.1in) directors had been put out of action and the automatic flak had been considerably reduced by the time that the first aircraft released its bombs at 0530. All released their bombs from a height of 3,000ft(900m) or less, which unfortunately gave the bombs insufficient time to reach the velocity required to penetrate the armour which they were intended to defeat. Nevertheless, of the 1,600lb(725.7kg) bombs released, three hit, as well as five 500lb(226.8kg) bombs; one 600lb(272kg) bomb burst in the air after hitting the funnel, and one 600lb(272kg) bomb burst under water and caused flooding of the starboard outboard spaces, abreast the after boiler room. The hits, like all but one of those which followed, were concentrated between 'B' and 'C' turrets, with the exception of one 500lb (226.8kg) bomb which penetrated the 2in(50mm) quarterdeck abreast 'D' turret and broke up on the outboard slope of the 4.7in(120mm) main-deck armour, where it caused a serious fire in a mess-deck. Other 500lb(226.8kg) bombs failed to penetrate the 2in(50mm) armour, and only one 1,600lb(725.7kg) bomb actually reached the armour deck, above the port engine room, and, having been released from 2,000ft (610m) by either 'F' or 'K' of 830 Squadron, it had insufficient velocity to do more than bulge the main armour. Nevertheless, this bomb caused serious damage, both from its blast and from the subsequent fire which was fed by petrol vapour from ruptured aircraft refuelling pipes. A 500lb(226.8kg) SAP bomb passed through a boat near the foot of the mainmast, penetrated the port aircraft hangar and exploded on the 2in(50mm) upper-deck in the wardroom, where another major fire developed.

A little farther forward, the 600lb(272kg) A/s bomb explosion crushed the port side of the funnel, and six of the twelve uptakes, and blew in the roof of the already damaged port hangar, causing a minor fire. Another 1,600lb(725.7kg) bomb passed through the roof of 's.1' 150mm (5.9in) turret, was deflected on penetrating the upper-deck, and exploded in the junior officers' quarters at the base of the funnel, causing another extensive fire.

During the first attack, the third 1,600lb(725.7kg) bomb hit, by-passed the armour deck by hitting underwater, below the 5.65in(145mm) lower belt, but then exploded outside the 1.75in(45mm) protected bulkhead, which was dished inwards over a length of 15ft(4.6m). The wing compartments flooded and there was a hole about 3ft(0.914m) deep and 18in(47.5mm) wide in the outer plating. The 600lb(272kg) A/s bomb which exploded about 10ft(3m) away from *Tirpitz*'s starboard side, caused substantially more damage than the larger direct hit underwater. Detonating at a depth of 30ft(9.1m)—below the belt armour—it dished the external plating to a maximum depth of 3ft(0.914m), over a length of 50ft(15.24m) and width of 16ft(4.9m), causing extensive damage to the frames and the starboard bilge keel. The plates were split (at a welding line) over a length of 50ft(15.24m), and the shock wave travelled up a sea water inlet pipe and caused more damage at the inboard end, under the boiler room.

One Barracuda was lost. 'M' of 830 Squadron, flown by Sub-Lieutenant(A) T. C. Bell, RNVR, with Sub-Lieutenant (A) R. N. Drennan, RNVR as Observer, and Leading Airman G. J. Burns as Telegraphist Air-Gunner, was last seen flying up Kaafjord in a controlled glide. Nothing further is known of the fate of this aircraft.

The bombing attack had lasted one minute. *Tirpitz* was left lying across the fiord, with her bows very close to the west shore, in thick smoke and without a tug visible at hand. The engines were intact, but the telegraphs were out of order, as was the helm indicator. As a result of the flooding of the outboard starboard wing compartments, the ship was listing slightly. 'As it was doubtful if the trials could be carried out . . . it was

decided to return to the net enclosure.' At 0636, *Tirpitz* was still trying to get back to her berth when the second wave of aircraft was reported.

The second strike took off from 0525—just as the first was attacking. The prolonged exposure of these Barracudas' engines to Arctic winds while on the passage north, caused the failure of one 829 Squadron aircraft to start, and 'Q' of the same squadron crashed into the sea shortly after take-off, with the loss of all members of the crew. This aircraft was carrying a 1,600lb(725.7kg) bomb, which meant that only two of these most important weapons were carried by this wave. The other 17 aircraft carried thirty-nine 500lb (226.8kg) SAP, nine 500lb(226.8kg) MC, and two 600lb(272kg) A/s bombs. The strike was led by Lieutenant-Commander (A) V. Rance, RN, No 52 TBR Wing Leader.

The strike followed the same pattern as the first—a low-level approach preceding a climb to cross the coast at 10,000ft(3,000m). The target area was clearly distinguishable from 40 miles away due to the brown smoke coming from the Kaafjord smoke screen.

The smoke-screen was more of a hindrance to *Tirpitz* than the attacking aircraft, obscuring her control positions but not masking the outline of the ship. All attempts at sound-detection after an initial air raid alert at 0633 were nullified by the ship's steam siren becoming jammed open. The 4.1in(105mm) flak fired a box barrage in the approach sector, but the close-range flak had to fire completely blind—a mode for which the automatic guns were neither intended nor equipped. The 10 Hellcats of 800 Squadron and the 20 Wildcats of 896 and 898 Squadrons were as effective against the flak as their predecessors had been, and again, only one Barracuda was lost—'M' of 829 Squadron, flown by Sub-Lieutenant (A) H. H. Richardson, RNVR, with Sub-Lieutenant (A) A. G. Cannon, RNVR and Leading Airman E. Carroll. Hit in the port wing during the attack, it flew north but was seen to crash en route to the coast.

Nothing was seen of the Barracudas' attack from the target, but five more hits were scored. One 1,600lb (725.7kg) bomb, released from 3,000-3,500ft(900-1,050m), penetrated the 2in(50mm) forecastle, but then fetched up against a supporting girder, where it lodged—unexploded. Two 500lb(226.8kg) bombs exploded on the upper-deck, causing only splinter damage, but one 500lb(226.8kg) SAP went through the roof of the starboard hangar and exploded near 's.1.' 5.8in(150mm) turret, causing another fire in close proximity to one started by a 1,600lb(725.7kg) bomb in the first attack. The fifth hit by the second wave was by a 500lb(226.8kg) SAP bomb which exploded as it was passing through the upper-deck, blowing a 6ft(1.8m) diameter hole and starting a large fire in the living quarters and stores below. 'P.I' turret was also put out of action by this hit. A near miss abreast the starboard propeller bracket caused minor splits and dishing around the bracket, with accompanying flooding.

Again, the attack was delivered swiftly and the aircraft returned to their carriers. The arrester hook on one Hellcat refused to lower, and the 800 Squadron pilot ditched safely alongside a destroyer. 'B' of 831 Squadron had been unable to release one 600lb(272kg) A/S bomb and was recovered last, aboard *Furious*. One 1,600lb(725.7kg) bomb had failed to release during the first strike, and an electrical fault in 'P' of 829 Squadron had meant that the three 500lb(226.8kg) SAP bombs carried by this aircraft had been released 'safe', but the other 37 aircraft had dropped 92 bombs, with a gross weight of 25 tons.

The fighters had not only confined themselves to attacks on *Tirpitz*, where flak mountings and directors had been riddled by 0.50in(12.7mm) armour-piercing hard-core shot. As the flak-suppression aircraft withdrew, they attacked small patrol craft and auxiliaries in Stjernsund, Langfjord, and off Loppa Island. The first wave straffed an armed trawler—*Vorpostenboot 6103*—and killed its Commanding Officer, wounded a man aboard a netlayer, and set on fire the 535ton steamer *Dollart* and, more important, the 13,246ton *CA Larsen*, a heavy repair ship, formerly a whale oil refinery ship. The second wave damaged a pair of U-Jaegers—*1212* and *1218*, of the local A/S patrol force, wounding another dozen men.

The casualties aboard *Tirpitz* were severe. No fewer than 120 officers and ratings were killed, as well as two civilian repair workers; another 316 were wounded, including the Captain, who was struck by splinters during the first attack. When it is remembered that no bomb penetrated the main armour, and only five bombs defeated the upper-deck armour, it is surprising that the casualties should have been so high—some 15 per cent of the ship's complement. Although the majority of the men hit were reported to have been guns' crews, the flak fired 506 rounds of 4.1in(105mm), 400 rounds of 37mm, and 8,260 rounds of 20mm in about five minutes firing time.

Tirpitz had sustained serious superficial damage, but she was still able to steam and fire her main armament. The damage underwater, caused by the attack on 3 April, took a month to repair, with divers carrying out welding in water near freezing point. Docking in Germany was not considered on this occasion, although it would have improved the quality of the repairs. The internal damage caused by blast and fire took rather longer to repair, as considerable lengths of telephone and electric cabling required replacement, but by 1 July 1944, *Tirpitz* was ready to commence trials once again—the Admiralty assessment of the effects of the damage had given the Germans three months to make her fit for action.

The work in Kaafjord proceeded unhindered, although this had not been the intention of the Admiralty. Three carrier strike operations were planned during the period, but all had to be cancelled due to the bad weather in the Altenfjord area. On 24 April, Operation 'Planet', involving the same carriers as 'Tungsten' with the exception of the substitution of *Striker* for *Fencer* as the A/S carrier, was cancelled as the force approached the flying-off position. On 15 May, 27 Barracudas actually took off from *Victorious* and *Furious*—the only carriers involved—for Operation 'Brawn'. The strike, escorted by Corsairs and Seafires, reached the coast, but found that there was solid cloud at 1,000ft(300m) over Kaafjord, and turned back. Finally, on 28 May, the same two ships abandoned Operation 'Tiger Claw' without launching a strike, and went to find better weather off Aalesund, where four large merchant ships were disposed of on 1 June.

Victorious left the Home Fleet after this operation, and there was a seven-week delay before two more Fleet carriers—*Formidable* and the brand-new *Indefatigable*—could finish their working up. No 8 TBR Wing transferred from *Furious* to *Formidable* and was replaced by 20 F6F-3 Hellcat Is of 1840 Squadron in the old carrier, while *Indefatigable* embarked No 9 TBR Wing (820 and 826 Squadrons), as well as 1770 Squadron, the first unit to become operational with the new Fairey Firefly two-seat fighter.

8
Operations 'Mascot' and 'Goodwood'

On 17 July, the three carriers launched a single strike, consisting of 21 Barracudas from *Formidable* and 23 from *Indefatigable*, with a top cover of 18 Corsairs, and a flak-suppression escort of 12 Fireflies and 20 Hellcats. All but two of the Barracudas were armed with 1,600lb(725.7kg) bombs, the others carrying three 500lb(226.8kg) MC bombs each. The strike left the area of the force at 0135 and approached to within 10 miles of Loppa Island before starting the climb to 9,000ft(2,750m). No cloud was seen during the outward flight, but on reaching the deployment point, 10 miles south-west of *Tirpitz*, it was seen that there was nearly half cloud cover over the head of Altenfjord and that an effective smoke-screen was rising to nearly 1,000ft(300m) over Kaafjord.

Since April, the German Navy had improved the radar warning stations and communications in the area, as well as increasing the smoke generating facilities. Nevertheless, the incoming strike was not detected until it was 43 miles away, at 0200, and the report took four precious minutes to reach *Tirpitz*. The smoke generators ashore and on the battleship's upper-deck were started at 0213, and within a minute, the cover was continuous and steadily thickening. The 380mm(15in) guns opened fire at 0219, followed almost immediately by the 150mm(5.9in) and 105mm(4.1in) batteries, firing a barrage in the direction of the strike's approach.

As a result of the dense smoke-screen, only two fighters and two No 9 Wing Barracudas actually sighted *Tirpitz*, and the 37 others which released their bombs on *Tirpitz* did so individually, over a period of some 25 minutes, using the flashes of the flak as aiming points. Seven near-misses were felt aboard the ship, which was severely shaken. One Barracuda bombed a flak battery on the shore, another dropped 500lb (226.8kg) bombs on a destroyer in Langfjord, and a third missed the tanker *Nordmark* with a 1,600lb (725.7kg) bomb. The fighters straffed flak positions up and down Altenfjord and forced *Vp 6307* (510 tons)

aground, to become a loss.

The flak was intense throughout the attack, and during the 33 minutes of firing, *Tirpitz* alone expended 39 rounds of 380mm(15in), 359 rounds of 150mm(5.9in), 1,973 rounds of 105mm(4.1in), 3,967 rounds of 37mm, and no less than 28,550 rounds from her eighty 20mm barrels. Several Barracudas were damaged, and one force-landed alongside *Formidable* on return, the crew being rescued, but the only loss in the target area was a Corsair. *Tirpitz* claimed to have destroyed 12 aircraft. It had been intended to repeat the strike, with a second wave which was to have been launched at 0800, but the follow-up was cancelled due to the approach of fog in the launching area.

Although it was known that no damage had been inflicted on *Tirpitz* by the 'Mascot' attack, she was left alone for another five weeks. However, with the resumption of Russian convoys in the autumn, it was decided that another major operation should be mounted and, that on this occasion, strikes should continue until substantial damage had been inflicted.

Formidable, *Furious* and *Indefatigable* sailed from Scapa Flow on 18 August 1944, in company with the escort carriers *Trumpeter* and *Nabob*, and a powerful screen which included the battleship *Duke of York* and three heavy cruisers. The strike squadrons were again changed, *Indefatigable* lending 826 Squadron to *Formidable* to fly with 828 Squadron, while *Furious* received her own No 8 TBR Wing back, having transferred the Hellcats of 1840 Squadron to *Indefatigable*. The Hellcat squadron and the Corsairs of *Formidable*'s No 6 Fighter Wing (1841 and 1842 Squadrons) had received dive-bombing training during the intervening period. The two escort carriers were armed with a dozen Grumman TBF-1C Avenger IIs and a flight of FM-1 Wildcats each; it was intended that the Avengers would undertake systematic minelaying in the openings of Altenfjord to the sea.

The first strike was to have been launched on 21 August, to cover the passage of convoy JW59 past Bear

Island, but bad weather in the target area caused postponement for 24 hours. At 1150 on 22 August, 32 Barracudas, 24 Corsairs, 11 Fireflies, nine Hellcat fighter-bombers, and eight Seafires (of *Indefatigable*'s No 24 Fighter Wing) took departure. On crossing the coast, solid cloud cover at 1,500ft(450m) obliged the Barracudas and Corsairs to return, in accordance with the orders. The Seafires continued to create a damaging diversion at Banak airfield and the Kolvick seaplane base, and the Fireflies and Hellcats delivered a 'teasing' attack on *Tirpitz*, descending below cloud, and following a road over the mountains to Kaafjord.

Tirpitz received little warning of the attack, and the smoke-screen was incomplete when the Fireflies began their flak-suppression runs at 1249, two minutes before the Hellcats attacked, each dropping a 500lb(226.8kg) SAP bomb. No hits were scored on the battleship, but again, other minor craft were badly damaged, including the U-boat *U 965* at Hammerfest. The seaplane anchorage at Bukta was also strafed and two of *Tirpitz*'s Ar 196As were destroyed on the water.

The minelaying operations were postponed due to the low cloud in Altenfjord, and were subsequently abandoned when first *Nabob* and then the frigate *Bickerton* were torpedoed by *U 354*, towards the end of the afternoon. The frigate was sunk, but *Nabob* managed to struggle back to Scapa Flow under her own steam, though she was badly damaged aft.

At 1830, *Indefatigable* flew off six Hellcat fighter-bombers and eight Fireflies, for another nuisance raid. Arriving over Langfjord at about 1910, they achieved complete surprise and not until the Fireflies began their anti-flak run did the smoke generators start functioning, although the flak had opened fire as the aircraft began their dives from 8,000ft(2,500m). The Hellcats scored several near-misses, but no hits on *Tirpitz*. During the withdrawal, all the fighters attacked shipping and radar stations, damaging the tankers *Jeverland* and *Nordmark* and the supply ship *Neumark*, as well as a picket vessel—*Vp 6504*—in the approaches to Altenfjord.

One Hellcat from the first strike had been shot down, as well as a Seafire over Banak, but there were no casualties in the evening. *Tirpitz* had expended 75 rounds of 380mm(15in), 487 rounds of 150mm(5.9in), approximately 2,000 rounds of 105mm(4.1in), 4,000 rounds of 37mm, and 30,000 rounds of 20mm, and claimed 12 aircraft shot down during the two attacks. One man was killed and ten wounded by the fighters' gunfire.

The escort carriers withdrew on the evening of 22 August, covered by *Formidable* and *Furious*, the latter requiring refuelling before she could continue to operate. *Indefatigable* was to have launched a diversionary attack on the tankers and destroyers in Langfjord on 23 August, but again bad weather forced abandonment.

Formidable and *Furious* rejoined on 24 August, and by 1500, the three carriers had flown off 33 Barracudas (all armed with 1,600lb(725.7kg) bombs), 24 Corsairs (five carrying one 1,000lb(453.6kg) A/P bomb each), 10 Hellcat fighter-bombers, 10 Fireflies, and eight Seafires, these last to attack Banak again. The launch position was farther to the south than usual, and the strike flew parallel to the coast to make a landfall for an approach from the south of Kaafjord. At 1535, German radar detected the strike heading south at a range of 63 miles, and passed the alarm to *Tirpitz* six minutes later. The target was thus well alerted, and the smoke-screen had developed by 1600, when the Hellcats and Fireflies attacked, five minutes ahead of the Barracudas and Corsairs.

The Hellcats scored their first hit in this attack, a 500lb(226.8kg) SAP bomb exploding on the roof of 'B' turret, destroying the quadruple 20mm mounted there, but merely denting the 5.1in(130mm) armour. The success cost the squadron two aircraft, including that flown by the Commanding Officer, Lieutenant-Commander A. R. Richardson, RNZNVR.

By the time that the Barracudas attacked, supported by all the Corsairs, *Tirpitz* was completely shrouded in smoke from above, forcing the bombers to release blindly, but in well co-ordinated attacks. The result was that there was an even dispersion of bombs dropped, from a height of 4,000–5,000ft(1,219–1,524m). One 1,600lb(725.7kg) bomb hit *Tirpitz*, just a few feet to port of the bridge, and thanks to the height of release it penetrated five decks, with a total thickness of 5.8in(150mm), before coming to rest in No 4 Switchboard Room, on the platform-deck. It failed to explode. German dissection of the bomb and fuze revealed not only that the latter had not functioned, but that the bomb had not been completely filled; it contained rather less than half of the 215lb(97.5kg) of explosive normal in this type of bomb. There is no doubt that, had the bomb functioned correctly, serious flooding would have resulted, as well as considerable structural damage.

One Corsair was shot down in Kaafjord, and another had to ditch on return, poor rewards for the expenditure of 72 rounds of 380mm(15in) and 510 rounds of 150mm(5.9in), as well as 40 per cent of the remaining automatic flak ammunition supply. Eight men had been killed and 13 wounded, but *Tirpitz* had, once more, escaped serious damage.

As usual, the fighters enjoyed free rein in the area,

severely damaging two more *Vorpostenboote—6502* and *6510*—a minesweeper and the radar station on Loppa Island. A bomb released at *Tirpitz* fell ashore and landed on a naval flak ammunition dump ashore, causing it to blow up; another bomb destroyed three guns of a heavy flak battery. The battleship's last Ar 196A was damaged beyond repair at Bukta.

A pair of Fireflies reconnoitred Kaafjord at 1930 on the same evening, taking photographs in order to assess damage. This stimulated the defences to make a smoke-screen and start an intense flak barrage.

Furious now withdrew, leaving a pair of Barracudas and a pair of Seafires to replace losses from *Indefatigable*. *Formidable* and '*Indefat*' were prevented from striking again by alternating days of gales and fog, up to 29 August. Even on that day the forecast was poor, but a strike was flown off from 15.30hrs. The strike consisted of 26 Barracudas, 17 Corsairs (two with 1,000lb(453.6kg) bombs), 10 Fireflies, seven Hellcats, and seven Seafires again bound for a diversionary attack. Four Hellcats were armed with 500lb(226.8kg) Target Indicator bombs, to mark the position of *Tirpitz* before the smoke-screen was fully developed, and give the Barracudas accurate aiming points.

Unfortunately, the radar stations on the outer islands had been tracking aircraft from the carriers throughout the day, these being the usual A/S patrols and fighter patrols. At 1640, a small formation of aircraft was detected 54 miles from Kaafjord—probably the Seafires heading for their attack on Hammerfest—and all chance of surprise was lost. The main attack did not begin for another 45 minutes, for owing to an inaccurate forecast of the wind between the carriers and *Tirpitz*, the main strike made its landfall too far to the south, and had to take a circuitous route to avoid cloud between the coast and the target.

The smoke-screen was the most effective yet encountered by Royal Navy aircraft, and all aircraft, including the 'Pathfinder' Hellcats, bombed blindly. Several near-misses shook *Tirpitz*, and six men were wounded by splinters and flash burns; the ammunition hoist of one 4.1in(105mm) flak mounting was damaged by a bomb fragment. Targets ashore were also bombed, and a fuel storage tank containing 350 tons of oil was hit and burned out. The fighters straffed the usual miscellany of ships, but inflicted no serious damage. One Firefly and one Corsair were shot down by *Tirpitz*, which fired 54 rounds from the main armament, 161 rounds of 150mm(5.9in), and up to 20 per cent of the diminishing lighter calibre stocks.

It was evident to the C-in-C Home Fleet that *Tirpitz* had not been immobilised, despite the expenditure of 52 tons of bombs in 95 sorties and 73 escort and support sorties, which had cost the carriers eight aircraft in the attacks on the battleship. In view of the risk, however slight, of intervention by *Tirpitz*, *Formidable* and *Duke of York* withdrew to the north, to cover the passage of RA59A, which had left the Kola Inlet on 28 August. *Tirpitz* was in no condition to attempt a sortie, however, because she was desperately short of flak ammunition. Additionally, the German Navy was aware of the determination of the carrier aircrew, who would welcome an opportunity to strike unhampered by smoke. Convoy RA59A was undisturbed by air and surface forces; one of the three U-boats destroyed by the convoy's escort (which included two escort carriers) was *U 354*, which had torpedoed *Nabob*.

During the entire series of carrier strikes, no fighter cover was provided for *Tirpitz*—a sad reflection on the lack of cooperation between the Luftwaffe and Kriegsmarine at every command level. With only her flak as defence against determined air attack, *Tirpitz*'s good fortune could not last very much longer.

9

The Ship Busters

Tirpitz repaired the minor damage caused by the Royal Navy's air attacks during the first half of September and once more made ready for full-power sea trials, which were programmed for 16 September. It will be recalled that the previous programme had had to be postponed because the Royal Navy had also chosen that day for activity in Altenfjord; unfortunately for *Tirpitz*, the Royal Air Force had already made the first moves preparatory to forcing complete cancellation of the trials.

Since the last Bomber Command attacks on *Tirpitz*, in April 1942, the RAF's main contribution had consisted of reconnaissance—maritime support and strategic—to keep track of the vessel's changes of anchorages, and to protect shipping against a surprise raid. After the failure of the Royal Navy to inflict crippling damage in August 1944, the Admiralty requested the Air Ministry to despatch heavy bombers armed with heavy bombs. Early in September, agreement was forthcoming and No 5 Group, Bomber Command, was ordered to plan and execute the raid.

An élite squadron, which specialised in the accurate delivery of ordnance on targets of particular strategic importance was ordered to lead the attack. This was the famous No 617 Squadron, popularly known as the 'Dam Busters' after their first, and probably most spectacularly successful, operation—the breaching of the Moehne and Eder dams in May 1943.

At one time, in 1943, it had been proposed to use a modified version of the 'dam buster' bomb against *Tirpitz*, but the terrain surrounding Kaafjord did not lend itself to the low-level approach required for the delivery of the weapon. Since June 1944, however, the squadron's Avro Lancaster Is had been delivering a 12,000lb(5,454kg) Medium Capacity bomb which had great penetration when dropped on concrete or natural surfaces, and which it was believed could penetrate thick armour plate without major loss of effect through deformation of the relatively light casing. The 5,100lb (2,318kg) Torpex charge would inflict catastrophic

damage if detonated inboard, and the mining effect from a near miss at 50ft(15m) depth would be considerable. An essential part of the Lancaster's delivery system was the stabilised automatic bomb sight, which added what was virtually a 'lead computing' gyroscope to the usual compensations for aircraft height and speed, wind velocity, air temperature and pressure, and 'bomb trail'. No 617 Squadron was the only unit operating with the SABS in the autumn of 1944, and to increase the size of the striking force, one of the most proficient of the squadrons equipped with the Mk XIV bombsight—No 9 Squadron—was also detailed. Like No 617, No 9 was equipped with Lancaster Is with specially bulged bomb-bays, first introduced in 1943 to accommodate a 12,000lb(5,454kg) High Capacity blast bomb.

Nos 617 and 9 Squadrons left Woodhall Spa and Bardney airfields on 10 September, refuelled at Lossiemouth, and set off for Yagodnik, 20 miles from Archangel and 600 miles from *Tirpitz*. The aircraft were all carrying the bombs destined for the battleship, and the fuel carried was only just sufficient for the Great Circle track which took them over Norway and northern Sweden. Without the assistance of the Russians, the range would have been too great for the Lancasters.

Eighteen aircraft from each squadron left Lossiemouth, but owing to the vagaries of the Earth's magnetic field and its effect on compasses, and also to the crews' lack of knowledge of the destination area, only 23 Lancasters actually arrived at Yagodnik at about dawn on 11 September; one of these had been damaged by AA fire while flying over Finland. Seven more arrived from various surrounding airfields and large fields during the day, but four aircraft of No 9 and two of 617 Squadron had to be left where they had forced-landed.

Bad weather prevented an attack from being mounted until 15 September, when 27 Lancasters took off shortly after dawn. Twenty-one were armed with the 12,000lb(5,433kg) MC bombs, and the remainder with twelve 400lb(181.8kg) 'JW II' buoyant bombs, which were intended to strike the water short of the target, and rise to explode against the unprotected bottom of the ship. Led by the Commanding Officer of 617 Squadron, Wing Commander J. B. Tait, DSO, DFC, the Lancasters approached Kaafjord from the south-east, descending from 16,000ft(4,800m) to 11,000ft(3,350m) during the last 30 miles of the run-up. *Tirpitz* had ample warning of the attack and, by the time that the first aircraft released their bombs, she was concealed by smoke.

The Lancasters had approached in groups of six, and during the run-up they closed to a tight formation, to give a small bomb pattern on the target. Only the first group—Tait's—was able to provide an aiming point for the SABS, but such was the accuracy of the sight that Tait's bomb hit *Tirpitz*, and those of his wingmen bracketed her. Subsequent groups of Lancasters missed by up to a mile, one pattern of JWs falling 1,700 yards(1,550m) to the south.

The bomb that hit did so right forward, just ahead of the anchor cable holders. It passed out through the ship's side and detonated below keel level close to the ship, about 35ft(10.6m) aft of the stem. A great hole 32ft(9.7m) deep by 48ft(14.6m) long, was blown in the starboard bow, and the ship's structure below the armoured deck was wrecked as far back as the transverse armoured bulkhead, 118ft(36m) from the stem; both the armoured and the upper-decks were bulged upwards, the former to a height of about 3ft(1m). Flooding was complete in the damaged area, and the draught forward increased by 8ft(2.4m)—wing compartments aft were flooded and fuel transferred aft to compensate the flooding forward, so that *Tirpitz* finished up with a total of 1,500 tons of sea water aboard.

Close near misses caused no flooding, but vibration and whip effect damaged the main propulsion machinery, which remained unserviceable for eight days. Many fire-control optical instruments were broken by the shock, and, as on other occasions when she was hit, her wireless aerials were broken from the masts. The crew were at action stations, so that casualties were slight, only five men being injured.

All 36 barrels of *Tirpitz*'s three main batteries—380mm(15in), 150mm(5.9in) and 105mm(4.1in)—and 98 guns ashore had provided a formidable barrage against the Lancasters, but all 27 bombers returned to Yagodnik, where they refuelled for the flight back to England on the following day.

No photographic reconnaissance of Kaafjord was possible until 20 September, when a Mosquito of No 540 Squadron brought back photographs of *Tirpitz*. Unfortunately, the battleship herself was in shadow,

but the photographic interpreters noticed discoloration of the forecastle, indicating damage. This was confirmed by agents' reports at a later date, but even these gave no indication of the full extent of the damage.

After examination of the bow, *Tirpitz*'s engineers came to the conclusion that nine months would be needed to rebuild the bow, provided that the work could be carried out without interruption. In the meantime, the ship was unseaworthy for operations, although her armament was intact and machinery repairs were soon completed. At a conference in Germany on 23 September, Doenitz and the SKL came to the conclusion that repairs were not possible, but that her armament would be of great value for defensive use. A defensive line was being prepared in the Lyngen-fjord area, to the west of Tromsö, and a berth was found for *Tirpitz* off Haakoy Island, about three miles to the west of the 'centre' of the town of Tromsö. A preliminary check on the anchorage indicated that in this berth there would be less than four feet(1.2m) of water below the battleship's keel, and that the bottom consisted of three feet(1m) of sand, on top of rock.

Tirpitz, her damaged bow held rigid by stringers welded across the hole in the starboard side, left Kaafjord on 15 October and arrived at her new berth on the next day. The damaged bow restricted speed to less than 10 knots, and powerful tugs were in attendance to assist with steering; the bow held and the tugs were not needed. Every available warship in northern Norwegian waters was included in the escort, for at such a slow speed, and deprived of her manoeuvrability, *Tirpitz* would have been an easy target for air or submarine attack.

Her departure was noticed by air reconnaissance, but there had been no indication of the purpose of the sortie, for there were no convoys at sea. Nevertheless, the Admiralty took the precautionary step of sailing the new Fleet carrier *Implacable*, at that time completing her work-up at Scapa Flow. *Implacable* sailed on 16 October, with 21 Barracudas of No 2 TBR Wing (828 and 841 Squadrons) and 11 Fireflies of 1771 Squadron embarked. During the forenoon of 18 October, the Fireflies were flown off 120 miles to the west of Tromsö in order to search for the battleship in the Tromsö area. On crossing the coast, four fighters were detached to attack Bardufoss airfield and a flying-boat base at Sorveisen, while the remainder searched for, and soon found, *Tirpitz*. Photographs were taken, not only of *Tirpitz* but also of the surrounding area—of great value in planning later attacks.

Implacable's Captain, L. D. Mackintosh, DSO, reported *Tirpitz*'s position to the C-in-C Home Fleet, and requested permission to launch a Barracuda strike.

To the great disappointment of the ship, this was forbidden: *Implacable*'s Seafire Wing had not been ready to embark when she sailed, and the only fighters available to provide top cover, flak suppression, and defensive protection for the carrier were the 11 Fireflies. With German fighters at Bardufoss, there was too great a risk to the Barracudas with so small an accompanying escort force.

1771 Squadron's photographs were not the first to reach the Admiralty. Not long after the Fireflies had flown over Haakoy, a Mosquito of No 540 Squadron had arrived from Leuchars and taken a set of good high-level photographs. The Mosquito was slightly damaged by flak, but returned direct to Leuchars, completing a round flight of just under 11 hours duration.

This out and back sortie from Scotland demonstrated the first of the two major disadvantages of the Haakoy anchorage. It was within the radius of RAF aircraft based in the United Kingdom. The second disadvantage was that the report of the surveyors regarding the nature of the anchorage was seriously in error. The minimum depth within the torpedo nets was 56ft(17m), not 40ft(12m), and the bottom was sand on soft mud—not rock, although the mud was not discovered until the end of October. The position of the ship could have been changed, but this would have meant that her main arcs of fire would not have been able to cover the seaward approaches to Tromsö. Instead, it was decided to fill in the sea bed around the ship to reduce the depth of water, an operation requiring the dumping of more than one million cu. ft (28,300cu. m) of rubble, using dredgers and hoppers. Before work could commence, Nos 617 and 9 Squadrons struck again.

With *Tirpitz* within reach of Lossiemouth, Bomber Command had ordered the two Lancaster squadrons to modify their aircraft by removing the mid-upper turret, installing fuselage tanks with 300 Imperial gallons(1,360litres) capacity, and by replacing the 1,460hp Rolls-Royce Merlin 22 engines with 1,620hp Merlin 24s. Thus altered, the Lancasters possessed the radius of action required and the power to get the overloaded aircraft safely off the ground.

The prevailing medium-level cloud over Tromsö dissipated with a change of wind on 28 October, and in the early hours of 29 October 32 Lancasters took off from 'Lossie' to attack *Tirpitz*. The raid did not achieve surprise and was greeted by the usual intense flak barrage, but no smoke-screen. Instead, the wind had changed back to the west, and cloud interfered with aiming from 13,000ft(3,950m), the minimum release height to achieve maximum penetration with the

12,000lb(5,454kg) MC bombs. The disappointed Lancaster crews persisted, making up to four runs apiece, but the nearest miss fell about 50ft(15m) to port of the rudders. During the withdrawal, one Lancaster was hit by flak, but made a forced-landing in Sweden.

Tirpitz suffered damage from the near-miss. The port side plating aft was split, and the glands at the outboard end of the port propeller shaft were distorted, allowing flooding along some 115ft(35m) of the port side aft. No 2 Steering Gear Compartment was flooded, the port shaft was bent and jammed, and the port rudder damaged. The bent shaft was repairable only in a dockyard; coupled with the damage to the bow, this latest blow had virtually immobilized *Tirpitz*, and, thereafter, she was referred to in official reports as 'Die Schwimmende Batterie'—the floating battery. Before transfer to Tromsö, her torpedo warheads had been landed, aviation fuel disembarked, and all aircraft ordnance removed. Now her complement was reduced, mainly in the engine room department, where only care and maintenance parties were retained, to keep steam available for the generators and to provide domestic services.

The End

Filling in the hole below *Tirpitz* began on 2 November and, by the evening of 11 November, the work was nearly half complete. The numerous not-so-near misses on 29 October had altered the contours of the surrounding sea bed, drawing attention to the true nature of the berth.

Shortly after midnight on 12 November 1944, 29 Lancasters of Nos 9 and 617 Squadrons took off from Lossiemouth to deliver their third attack. The outward trip was not made in formation, and aircraft made individual landfalls on the Norwegian coast to the south of Tromsö to take advantage of known gaps in the air warning radar cover. The first was reported to *Tirpitz* at approximately 0800, having crossed the coast near Bodö. Another three were reported to have crossed near Mosjoen at 0738, the report reaching Haakoy at 0815, and the AA defence officer informed the Luftwaffe at Bardufoss that an attack was probable. Fighter cover was requested at 0825, but for some reason, the Luftwaffe commander did not permit the aircraft to take-off.

The bombers rendezvoused to the south-east of Tromsö between 0830 and 0845, and were detected by *Tirpitz*'s radar as they made their approach in small groups, at between 12,500ft(3,270m) and 16,500ft(5,000m). Detection was at 0905, when the Lancasters were still 75 miles distant; the ship had been at action stations since 0900, but repeated

42

requests for fighter cover met with no response until 0915, when Bardufoss called to announce that fighters could not take off as Lancasters were over-flying the airfield! Ten minutes later, Bardufoss announced that one fighter had taken off and that more would follow—nothing was seen of these aircraft.

At 0927, the first group of bombers was sighted at about 25 miles to the south-east. No smoke genera-tors were operative on board the ship, and the shore system was not so effective as it had been in the steep narrow confines of Kaafjord, and it failed to provide any protection for *Tirpitz*. 'A' and 'B' 380mm(15in) turrets opened fire at 0938, with the Lancasters 13½ miles distant. The 150mm(5.9in) and 105mm(4.1in) guns joined in at 9½ miles, but without deterring the formations, which closed up as the range decreased.

The first group of Lancasters, led by Wing Comman-der Tait, released their bombs at 0941, and scored two direct hits, one to port of 'B' turret and the other on the port side amidships, entering the ship through the catapult track and exploding as it passed through the armoured deck over the port boiler room. The effects of the hit near the turret are not exactly known, but the other bomb tore a hole in the ship's side from the bilge keel to the upper-deck, torpedo bulkhead, armour, and all, over a length of some 45ft(14m). The Port No 1 Boiler Room, Centre Boiler Room, and Port Engine Room spaces flooded immediately, causing a heel to port of between 15° and 20°. A near miss off the bows added to the existing damage in that area, but by that stage, such damage was irrelevant.

During the next three minutes, a third 12,000lb (5,433kg) bomb hit on the port side, abreast 'P.III' 150mm(5.9in) turret, and another bomb near-missed abreast 'P.II' turret. The latter, opened Port No 2 Boiler Room and 'P.II' magazine and shell room, while the hit, opened 'P.III' magazine and shell room, a gyro compartment, and a fan room to the sea. Two hundred and twenty feet (67m) of the port side midships section of *Tirpitz* was now flooded from the double bottoms to the waterline, which had reached the upper-deck as she continued to roll to 40°. At about 0945, when she had reached this angle, the Captain, *Kapitän zur See* Junge, ordered the lower-decks to be evacuated. The volume of heavy flak had decreased considerably due to the heavy personnel casualties as well as the damage, but the starboard turrets and mountings were still in action, as were all serviceable automatic mount-ings—even though the Lancasters were beyond their effective range.

The heel increased and, by 0950 had reached nearly 70°. A fire had apparently been started by the hit near 'P.III' turret, and this reached the 'C' turret

magazine, for, at 0950 there was a major explosion which blew the turret out of its barbette. Two minutes later, *Tirpitz* capsized completely, and came to rest on the bottom, having rolled through 135°. Had the water been as shallow as had been intended, and the bottom firmer, her progress would have been arrested, and such armament as remained intact could have been used defensively.

The pall of smoke and steam created by the first hits had obscured the target for the last groups to bomb, but more than half the bombs fell within 250 yards (228m) of *Tirpitz*, including one on Haakoy, the crater of which much impressed the Germans. No Lancasters were lost.

Casualties aboard *Tirpitz* were severe. In spite of the Captain's order to evacuate the interior of the ship, many men had not been able to reach the upper-deck before she capsized, seven minutes later. Including those killed by the explosions of the bombs, the dead and missing totalled over 1,000 men. Many were trapped inside the ship, but 85 of these were later rescued by teams of workers cutting through the shell plating of the outer bottom on the exposed starboard side.

There were many boards of enquiry and post-mortems to establish the reasons for the capsizing, the reason for the large loss of life, and the reason for the lack of fighter protection. A genuine, but unpardonable, error had been made in the selection of the berth, which had led to the capsizing and, consequently, loss of life; but the last was beyond the control of the Navy. The Luftwaffe had never provided *Tirpitz* with the protection to which she was entitled as 'Queen on the Arctic Ocean chessboard'. Thirteen air attacks had been made on the battleship between January 1942 and November 1944, by 600 British aircraft—approxi-mately 390 naval and 200 RAF—and numerous reconnaissance aircraft had overflown her various anchorages. The only aircraft to be attacked by German aircraft had been the shadowing Albacores on 9 March 1942, when the defending 'fighter' had been *Tirpitz*'s own floatplane.

This one battleship had seriously limited the scope of operations of the British Home Fleet since January 1942, simply by sitting threateningly in Norwegian fiords. Promise far exceeded performance, for although the possibility of a sortie forced the Royal Navy to maintain overwhelming strength in Home Waters, calling upon the United States Navy for reinforce-ments—battleships, carriers (*Wasp* and *Ranger*, in 1942 and 1944), and cruisers, when *Tirpitz* did sail for offensive duties, the results were insignificant. The greatest German victory in the Arctic—the destruction of PQ17—had been achieved by simply repositioning *Tirpitz*.

Unfortunately, the Luftwaffe had claimed that victory as their own, thus reinforcing Reichsmarshall Herman Goering's conviction that the air force which he had built needed neither assistance from, nor to give assistance to, the Navy which he had deprived of its own air force. Lip-service was paid to Hitler's insistence on the provision of adequate air forces in northern Norway, but few practical steps were taken. Given this freedom, the agents of destruction—the Lancaster squadrons—carried out their task with thoroughness.

As stated at the very beginning, no warship is built in a vacuum, and *Tirpitz* was not intended to be the last of the line in German naval service. In May 1938, Hitler followed the Kaiser in deciding to build a fleet to equal that of the British Empire. The 'Z-Plan', drawn up in May 1938, called for the construction of six 56,200-ton battleships and three 32,300-ton battlecruisers, the last of which was to be in service by 1945. The new battleships were to have been armed with eight 406mm(16in) guns in twin turrets, and were virtually enlarged versions of *Tirpitz*, but with a marginally lower maximum speed. The battlecruiser design was for a 33½-knot ship with three 380mm(15in) twin turrets; three of these turrets were to be refitted into *Scharnhorst* and *Gneisenau*.

This plan was conceived in a vacuum, however, for its basic assumption was that war with Britain was unlikely before 1944, and the superiority was projected upon a comparison between the projected German Fleet and the existing and publicly forecast British Fleet in 1937. The Royal Navy also had plans for bigger battleships, each armed with nine 16in(406mm) guns, and four of these were approved in 1938 and 1939, completion being expected in 1942–44. The line-up at the forecast date for war would therefore have been:

GERMANY	BRITAIN
6 new battleships ('H'–'N')	4 new *Lion* class
2 *Bismarck* class	5 *King George V* class
3 new battlecruisers ('O'–'Q')	
2 *Scharnhorst* class	
= 48 x 16in(406mm), 46 x 15in(380mm)	= 36 x 16in(406mm), 50 x 14in(356mm)

The German Navy thus possessed an edge in post-1936 capital ships, but the Royal Navy had its three battlecruisers (*Hood*, *Renown* and *Repulse*), with 20 x 15in (380mm) guns between them; *Renown* had been completely modernised, *Repulse* partly so and *Hood* would have been re-armoured between 1940 and 1942, according to the programme. If these ships were not sufficient, there were still *Rodney* and *Nelson*, slower than the new battleships, but well armoured and armed with nine 16in(406mm) guns each; these ships, like the five 15in(380mm)-gunned *Queen Elizabeth* and three of the inferior 'R' class, were earmarked for use in the Far East and Mediterranean, against the Japanese and Italian Navies, but could be used most effectively to protect shipping against battlecruiser raids.

The principal British advantage lay not in the 9:8 ratio of line-of-battle ships, but in the possession of greater numbers of aircraft carriers: by 1944, the fleet would include seven modern ships, six of them with armoured decks, with a total complement of 324 aircraft. Against this, Germany had planned for only two carriers, with 84 aircraft between them.

All the plans were, in practice, little more than pipe-dreams; of the big battleships, only two German and two British ships were ever laid down, to be cancelled in 1940 and 1944 respectively, the former because the armour plate was needed for tanks, and the latter because of labour and material shortages in the hard-pressed shipyards. The German battlecruisers were never laid down, but one of the two carriers was completed to flight-deck level, and the other was under construction when work was suspended in the spring of 1940. All six of the British armoured fleet carriers of the 1936–39 Programmes were completed, five of them undertaking operations against *Tirpitz* in 1944.

It is idle to speculate as to what might have happened had the outbreak of war been delayed until the 1938 plans had been fulfilled—with more ships in hand, Hitler might have allowed the SKL to pursue a more aggressive course against the British Fleet. Given the desire of both Naval Staffs to decide the issue of Jutland once and for all, there might have been a set-piece battle, instead of the three actions which cost Germany two capital ships and Britain, one. In the war that was fought out, Hitler and the SKL between them prevented the concentration of force available, except for a brief period in 1943, in Norway. The result was that *Bismarck*, *Tirpitz* and *Scharnhorst* all perished alone, when together they might have survived and played a militarily positive role in challenging Allied sea power, instead of merely attempting to divert Allied attention.

Map section

Artwork by Chris Brown

500   0   500   1500

METRES (APPROX)

⚐ APPROXIMATE POSITIONS OF
    FLAK BATTERIES

N

2600 FT

ALTA
FJORD

KAA FJORD

BARBRUDALEN·
ANCHORAGE

1400 FT

ALTA

N O R W A Y

The Kaafjord Anchorages

Operation 'Sportpalast'

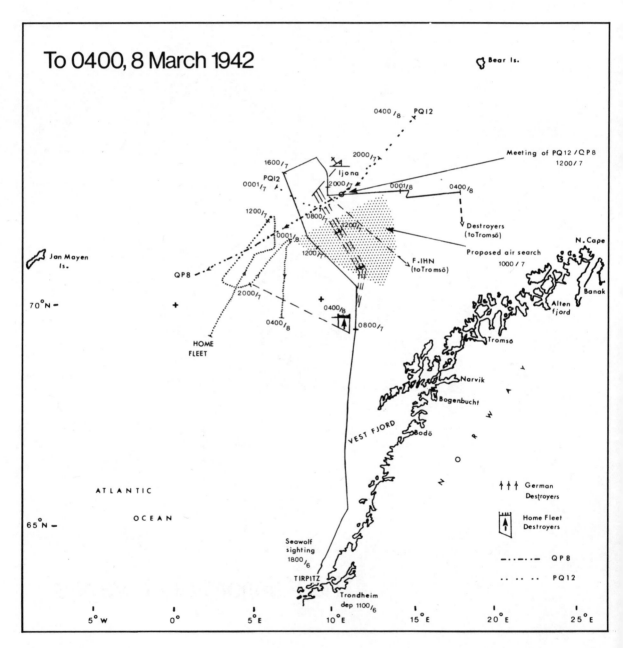

To 0400, 8 March 1942

Bear Is.

0400/8 PQ12

2000/7

1600/7
PQ12
0001/7

Ijona
2000/7

Meeting of PQ12/QP8
1200/7

0001/8

0400/8

Destroyers
(to Tromsö)

0800/7

1200/7

1200/7

Proposed air search
1000/7

F.IHN
(to Tromsö)

Jan Mayen
Is.

QP8

N. Cape

Banak

70°N

2000/7

0400/8

0001/8

0400/8

0800/7

Alten
fjord

Tromsö

HOME
FLEET

Narvik

Bogenbucht

Bodö

VEST FJORD

ATLANTIC

65°N

OCEAN

↑↑↑ German
Destroyers

Home Fleet
Destroyers

Seawolf
sighting
1800/6

— · — · — QP 8

· · · · · · PQ12

TIRPITZ

Trondheim
dep 1100/6

5°W   0°   5°E   10°E   15°E   20°E   25°E

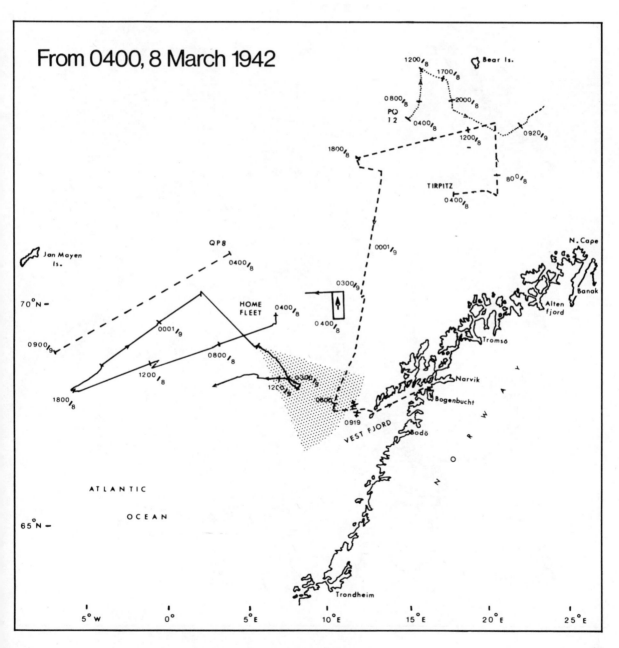

From 0400, 8 March 1942

Bear Is.

1200/8
1700/8
0800/8
PQ
12
0400/8
2000/8
1200/8
0920/9

1800/8

TIRPITZ
80°/8
0400/8

0001/9

N. Cape

QP8
Jan Mayen
Is.
0400/8

Banak

70°N —

0300/9
0400/8

HOME
FLEET   0400/8

Alten
fjord

0001/9

Tromsö

0900/9

0800/8
1200/8
0300/9
1200/9
0600/
0919

Narvik
Bogenbucht

1800/8

VEST FJORD
Bodö

N   O   R   W   A   Y

ATLANTIC

OCEAN

65°N —

5°W   0°   5°E   10°E   15°E   20°E   25°E

Trondheim

47

Convoy Operations PQ17, PQ18 and QP14

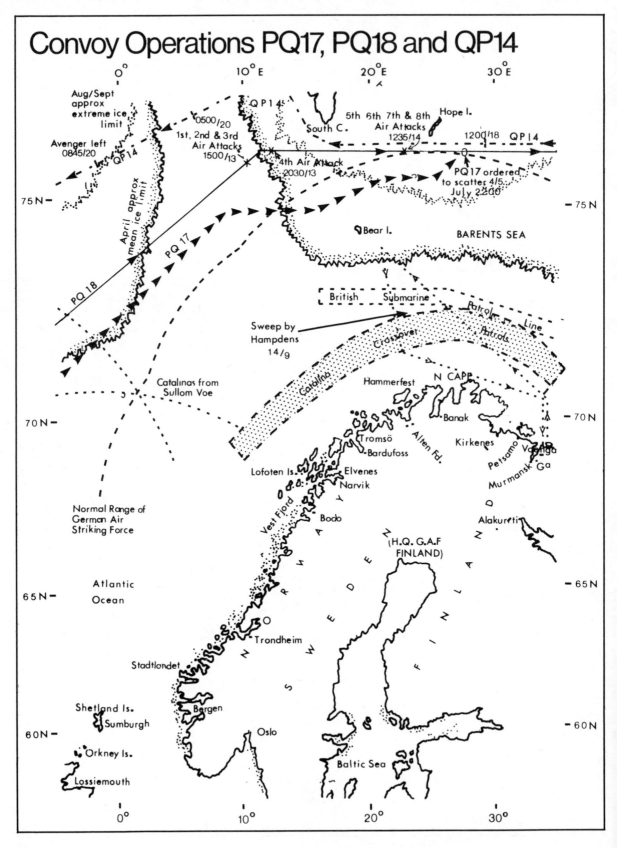

0°

10° E

20° E

30° E

Aug/Sept
approx
extreme ice
limit

Avenger left
0845/20

QP14

0500/20

1st, 2nd & 3rd
Air Attacks
1500/13

QP14

South C.

5th 6th 7th & 8th
Air Attacks
1235/14

Hope I.

1200/18   QP14

4th Air Attack
2030/13

PQ17 ordered
to scatter 4/5
July 2200

75 N

— 75 N

April approx mean ice limit

Bear I.

BARENTS SEA

PQ 17

PQ 18

British   Submarine   Patrol   Line

Sweep by
Hampdens
14/9

Crossover   Patrols

Catalina

N CAPE

Catalinas from
Sullom Voe

Hammerfest

70 N

— 70 N

Banak

Tromsö

Bardufoss

Alten Fd.

Kirkenes

Petsamo Vaenga

Lofoten Is.

Elvenes

Murmansk Ga.

Narvik

Normal Range of
German Air
Striking Force

Vest Fjord

Bodo

Alakurtti

(H.Q. G.A.F
FINLAND)

Atlantic
Ocean

65 N

— 65 N

Trondheim

Stadtlandet

Shetland Is.

Sumburgh

Bergen

Oslo

60 N

— 60 N

Orkney Is.

Lossiemouth

Baltic Sea

0°

10°

20°

30°

Profiles and plan

by Alan Raven

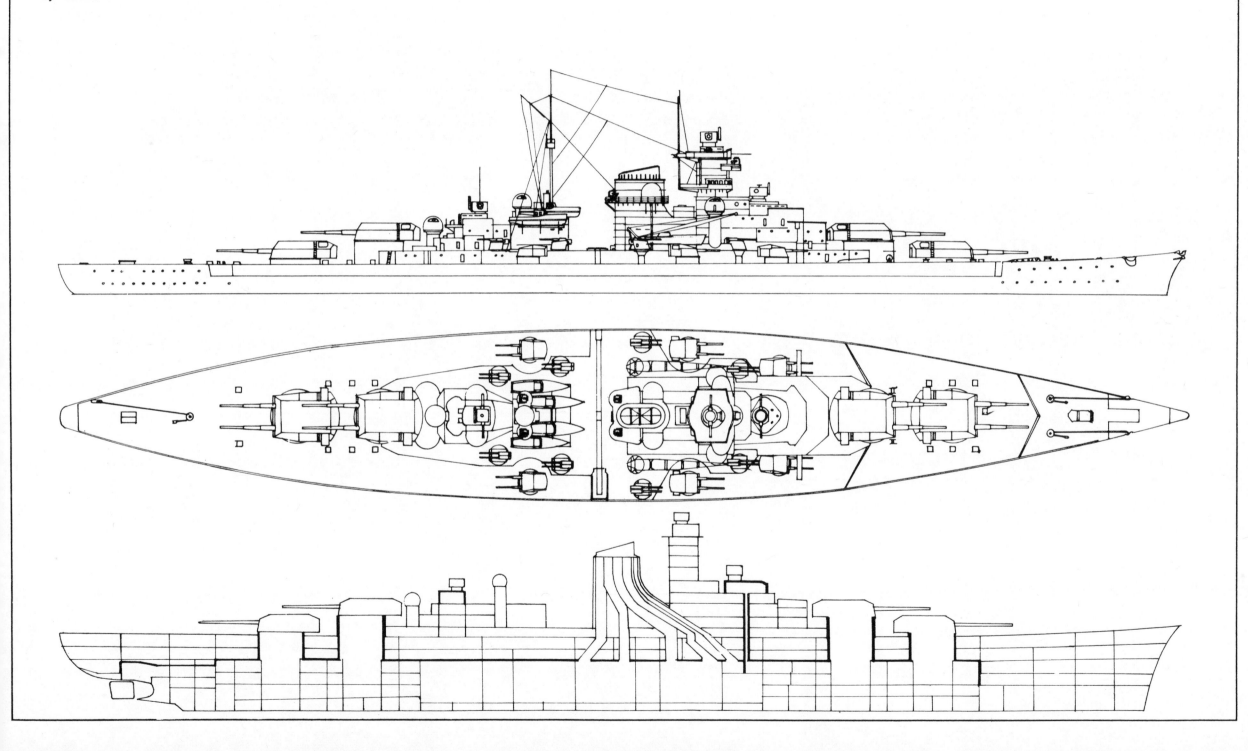

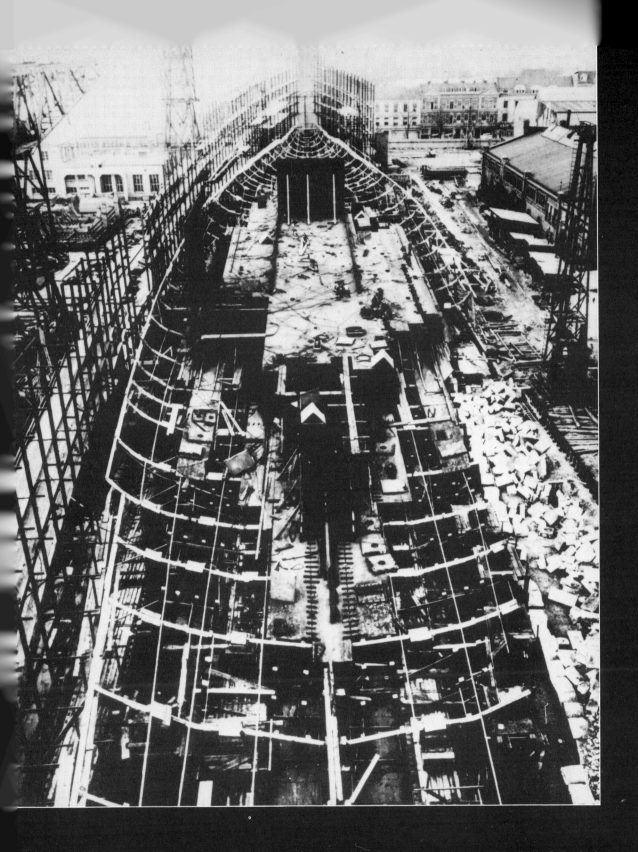

. The frame of the battleship takes shape on the biggest slipway at the Wilhelmshaven yard early in 1937. (*Tirpitz* Collection)

3

2, 3. *Gneisenau* as she and her sister-ship *Scharnhorst* appeared when first commissioned, and following their first Atlantic cruise together early in 1939, when the bow was extended and given a pronounced sheer, and the single funnel was topped with a raked cowl. The top of the 13in armoured belt, extending between 'A' turret and 'Y' turret, is clearly highlighted forward and aft. (*Tirpitz* Collection)

4. *Richelieu*, completed for sea trials as the German Army was over-running France, was unusual in that her 15in guns were concentrated in just two turrets, both mounted forward, while her 6in secondary armament was concentrated aft of the single large funnel. (Author's Collection)

5. *Littorio*, seen here off Sicily on 10 September 1943, after surrendering, was completed in August 1940, at which time her armament of nine 15in guns was exceeded in weight of broadside by only two British battleships—*Nelson* and *Rodney*—both of which were at least 5 knots slower. (Author's Collection)

5

6

7

6. Britain's *King George V* Class was originally to have been armed with twelve 14in guns, but this armament was reduced to ten guns in two quadruple and one twin turrets in an attempt to remain within the 35,000-ton limits. As can be seen in this view of HMS *Duke of York*, all superstructure was grouped in two blockhouse-like 'islands', separated by the aircraft catapult track, giving a squat appearance which contrasted with the tower or pyramid structures favoured by the other nations. (Ministry of Defence RN)

7. *Bismarck*, *Tirpitz*'s short-lived sister-ship, as she appeared when first commissioned in the autumn of 1940. (Author's Collection)

8. The last class of '35,000-ton' battleships to enter service were the US Navy's *North Carolina*s, the name ship of which commissioned in August 1941. Although armed with nine 16in guns in three turrets, they were relatively lightly armoured. USS *Washington* served with the British Home Fleet during the spring and summer of 1942. (US Navy)

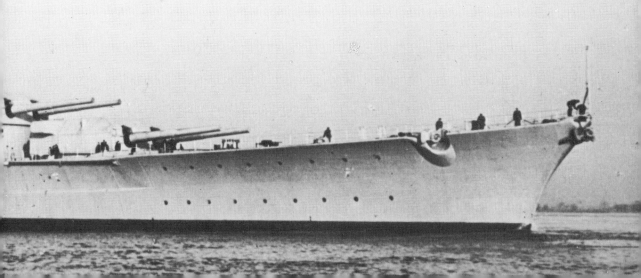

9. Keel-laying: 30 October 1936 at Wilhelmshaven Navy Yard. (*Tirpitz* Collection)

10. Wilhelmshaven Naval Yard workers receive a word of encouragement from Admiral Förster after the keel had been laid on 3 October 1936. (*Tirpitz* Collection)

11. *Tirpitz* with her main armoured deck completed. The barbettes for 'A' and 'Y' 15in turrets have been built as far as the upper-deck level, as have those for Nos 1 and 3 5.9in turrets port and starboard, while the octagonal hole in the foreground marks the site of 'X' barbette. The inclined armour outboard of the machinery spaces is plainly visible abaft 'S.2' barbette. (*Tirpitz* Collection)

12. The hull approaching readiness for launching, early in 1939. In the dry dock in the left foreground is a Leberecht *Maas* Class destroyer. (*Tirpitz* Collection)

11

12

13

13. Der Führer arrives in Wilhelmshaven for the launching ceremony on 1 April 1939. (*Tirpitz* Collection)

14. After a rally and address to Party members, Hitler enters the Dockyard. (*Tirpitz* Collection)

15. The launching ceremony was performed by Frau von Hassel, the daughter of von Tirpitz and the wife of a leading diplomat. Frau von Hassel at first demurred when asked to launch the ship, but pressure was applied and she complied, in spite of her distaste for Hitler's régime. (*Tirpitz* Collection)

16. The champagne splashes against the bows, and two workmen pull the cover off the ship's coat of arms. (*Tirpitz* Collection)

17. Technical hitch: the champagne has drained away but the ship has not yet moved. (*Tirpitz* Collection)

14

15

16

17

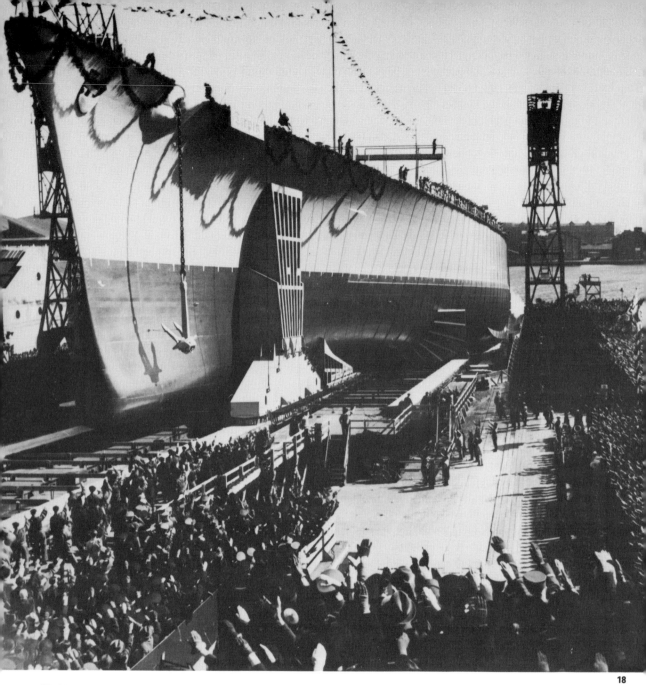

18. Moving at last, *Tirpitz* leaves the ways, saluted by most of the onlookers. (*Tirpitz* Collection)

19. The launch seen from a vantage point on the other side of the basin. (*Tirpitz* Collection)

20. 1 April 1939: tugs prepare to swing *Tirpitz* around immediately after the launch. (*Tirpitz* Collection)

19

20

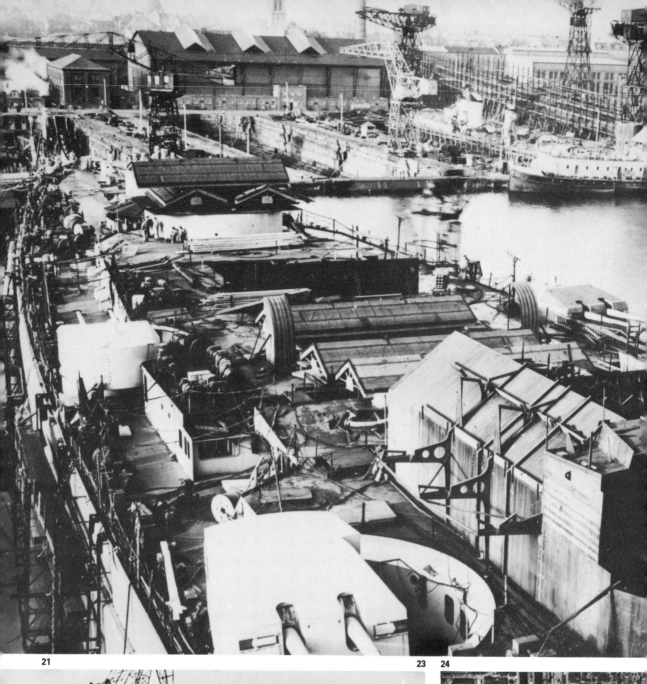

21

23 **24**

22

21. Fitting out: the superstructure begins to take shape. The arched-roofed structure immediately inboard of the nearer 5.9in turret is the forward starboard aircraft hangar, which has boat cradles attached to the roof and side. The circular aperture ahead of the hangar is to accommodate the starboard flak director. The ship under construction on *Tirpitz*'s old slip had not been positively identified, but is possibly the cancelled light cruiser 'M' (*Tirpitz* Collection)

22. The funnel is lifted into position, having been prefabricated in another corner of the Dockyard; The outer casing has not yet been fitted, but the searchlight and light flak platforms are in place. Note the thickness of the armour of 'X' turret's barbette. (*Tirpitz* Collection)

23. With turrets in place, *Tirpitz* appears to lack only the 15in guns and the armament directors. (*Tirpitz* Collection)

24. *Tirpitz*, seen through the lens of an RAF reconnaissance camera, lying in the rectangular fitting-out basin at Wilhelmshaven during the summer of 1940, her bows pointing towards the lock gates. The light cruiser *Nürnberg* lies alongside the adjacent wall, and there are two destroyers present, one across the basin from *Tirpitz* and the other in the dry dock immediately astern. (Crown Copyright)

25, 26. The 38cm 47-calibre Seekanone C/34 are lifted off their cradles for mounting aboard *Tirpitz*. Like all other large-calibre guns of the period, these were built by Krupps, the only German armaments firm having the specialized plant necessary for the manufacture of such weapons. (*Tirpitz* Collection)

27. The cluttered bridge structure of *Tirpitz* is in strong contrast with the 'blockhouse' appearance of British battleships, and the clean tower of the American battleships of the same period. Note the exposed searchlight on the funnel sponson, and the deliberate positioning of the main director to hide the radar antenna. (*Tirpitz* Collection)

25

26

30

28, 29. *Tirpitz* was commissioned on 23 December 1940, under the command of Kapitän zur See Karl Topp, seen inspecting a Division of his ship's company before the ceremony of hoisting the ensign. (*Tirpitz* Collection)

30. The Wardroom was situated under the after hangar, on the first deck. The false deck-hand, to left and right of the picture, conceals the usual maze of pipes and ventilation trunking. (*Tirpitz* Collection)

31. Grossadmiral Alfred von Tirpitz, architect of the Imperial German Navy of the First World War. This painting hung in the battleship's Wardroom. (*Tirpitz* Collection)

31

32. 'Stand-easy' in the Sickbay, a vast, airy space located immediately abaft 'Bruno' turret. The individual ear-phones and the wooden gimballing cots are in marked contrast with British and American practice of the day, where wood was a fire risk and two tiers of metal bunks were needed to deal with the number of casualties a battleship's huge crew might suffer in action. (*Tirpitz* Collection)

33. The ship's doctors take the air on the quarterdeck (fantail) as the ship lies in Wilhelmshaven Roads. (*Tirpitz* Collection)

34. The ship's Dispensary with the usual array of chemist's jars barred in to prevent them from being dislodged by vibration or the movement of the ship at sea. (*Tirpitz* Collection)

35. The Medical Department also boasted an X-ray unit, a necessary refinement in view of *Tirpitz*'s later isolated existence. (*Tirpitz* Collection)

36, 37, 38. The 'Toothwright's Workshop'—the dentist at work in his surgery, assisted by a Dental Sickbay Attendant in a somewhat scruffy overall. The dentist was unusual in that he also qualified as a diver while serving aboard *Tirpitz*. (*Tirpitz* Collection)

32

33

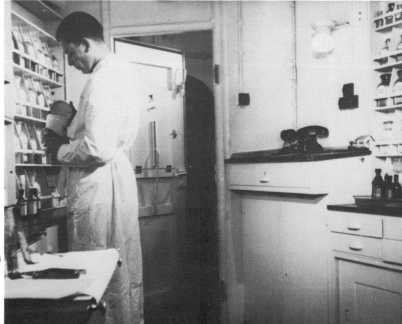

34

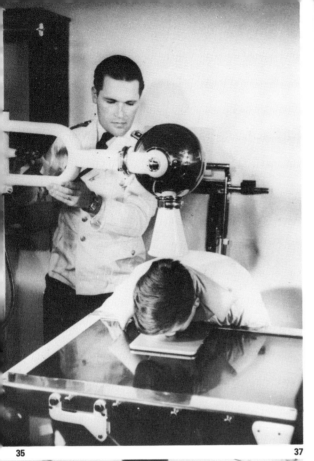

35

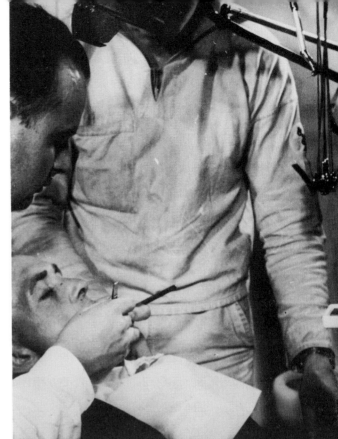

37

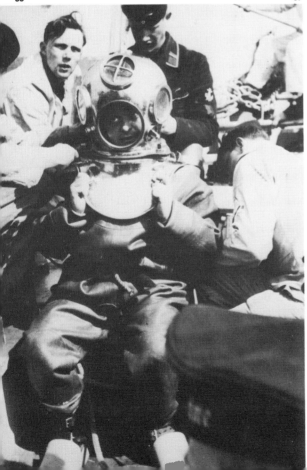

36

38

39. The Engineering Officer and his two assistants. The object outboard of the guardrail is a waste disposal chute (known as a 'gash chute' in the Royal Navy). (*Tirpitz* Collection)

40. Stokers perch on top of the funnel during a break from the dirty and unpleasant job of cleaning the boiler uptakes. (*Tirpitz* Collection)

41. The machinery control position in the centre engine room, showing the propeller revolution counters, telegraphs, and an array of linear gauges in place of the more common circular gauges. (*Tirpitz* Collection)

42. The Laundry, with a pressing machine on a scale appropriate to the size of the ship. (*Tirpitz* Collection)

39

41

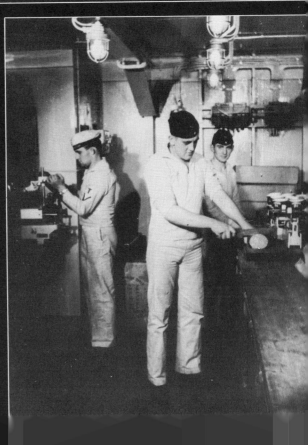

3. The Cold Room: carcasses and assorted würste are hung in one of the victual store-rooms, together with barrels of soused herring. (*Tirpitz* Collection)

4. The fare being prepared by the chefs appears meagre compared to the promise of plenty in the Cold Room. (*Tirpitz* Collection)

5. The Bakery: as in the case of the dental assistant, the cleanliness of the working rig does not seem to be adequate for the surroundings. (*Tirpitz* Collection)

6. The Chief Cook samples the broth. (*Tirpitz* Collection)

7. Mail, an important feature in maintaining morale aboard ship, required an organization equal to that of a small urban post office, handling letters and parcels to and from 2,000 men, in addition to the mass of routine official correspondence. (*Tirpitz* Collection)

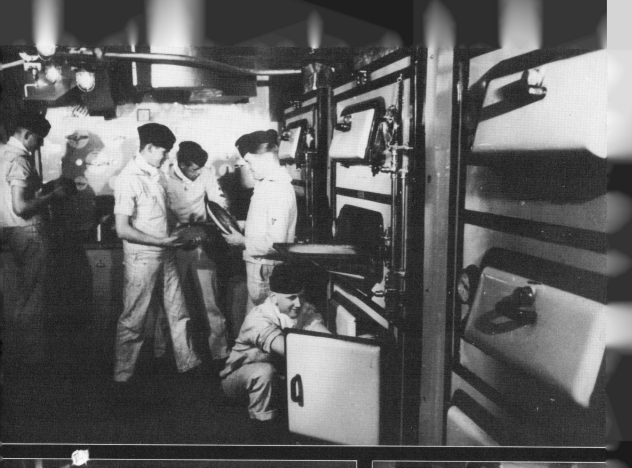

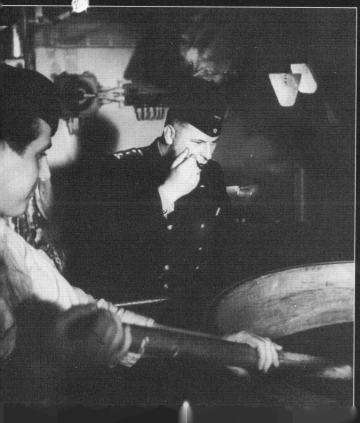

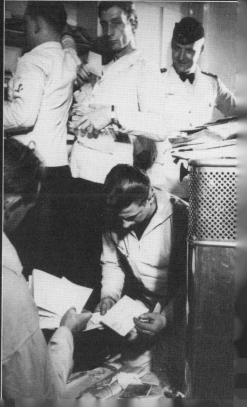

48. The ship's band poses on the quarterdeck; the drums are adorned with the ship's badge, as well as the naval ensign. (*Tirpitz* Collection)

49. Like most big ships, *Tirpitz* produced her own daily newspaper, using a small printing press. Here, one of the operators sets type, with a 'page' being laid out at bottom right. (*Tirpitz* Collection)

50. The finished product—'The Searchlight', with the enigmatic headline 'Stage-fright in Gibraltar'. (*Tirpitz* Collection)

51. The Shop, corresponding to the Royal Navy's Naafi Canteen, where ratings could buy cigarettes, postcards, writing materials and 'penny dreadfuls'. (*Tirpitz* Collection)

52. Relaxation in the beer bar. (*Tirpitz* Collection)

48

51

53. Kapitän Topp presents the trophy for the most efficient Division—a prized but perhaps unwieldy object to be stowed in a crowded mess-deck. (*Tirpitz* Collection)

54. The Officer of the Watch and his 'Side Party', the Bosun's Mate and two Quartermasters; this team was stationed on the quarterdeck while the ship was at anchor or alongside, controlling access to the ship and running the day-to-day routine. This photograph was taken while the ship was in Norwegian waters in 1942, apparently during an air-raid alert. (*Tirpitz* Collection)

55, 56. Storing ship at Wilhelmshaven before proceeding to sea for trials and the work-up. (*Tirpitz* Collection)

53

54

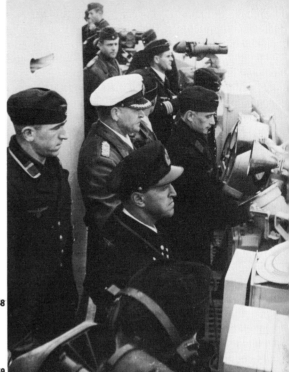

58

59

57. Ready for sea at last, *Tirpitz* gets under way in the Jade Roads in March 1941. (*Tirpitz* Collection)

58. *Tirpitz* anchored in the Jade River before her sea trials. Careless manipulation of the fuel oil sprayers has resulted in the emission of thick black smoke. The consequence could be a thick deposit of soot on deck or — more grievously — betrayal of the ship's position. (*Tirpitz* Collection)

59. Kapitän Topp on the cramped navigating bridge. Behind him and his numerous staff is the armoured conning-tower, the command station in action. (*Tirpitz* Collection)

60. A View of *Tirpitz*'s 'Caesar' and 'Dora' turrets, during the intial sea trials in the spring of 1941. The aftermost AA director has not yet been mounted, and the after conning-tower has only a short range-finder fitted. Four 20mm pedestals are visible (to port and starboard of 'D' turret, and on the deck between the upper and lower 37mm AA guns) but the AA gun barrels have been removed, possibly for workshop maintenance. (*Tirpitz* Collection)

60

61. *Tirpitz* at speed while undergoing trials in the Baltic. Although the 37mm flak abaft 'B' turret is protected from the weather, no protective tompions are fitted in the bore of the main armament barrels. (*Tirpitz* Collection)

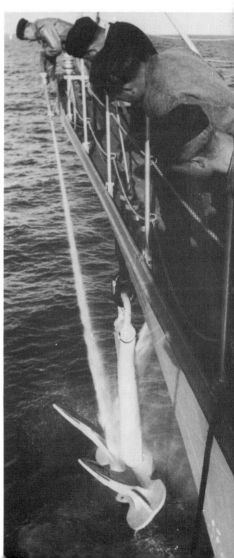

62. Hosing the Baltic silt off the anchor as the ship gets under way for the day's trials. (*Tirpitz* Collection)

63

64

63. "Can you hear me at the rear?"—a working party is detailed off. (*Tirpitz* Collection)

64. Swabbing down the decks, one of the oldest of shipboard chores. (*Tirpitz* Collection)

65, 66. Refuelling at sea: *Tirpitz* is being replenished by the 'Astern Method' whereby buoyant hoses from the tanker were picked up by the receiving ship and connected to the ship's own fuel lines on the forecastle. The 'tug o' war team' are seen hauling in the starboard hose from the tanker, while the port receiving hose is laid out by the anchor cable forelead. (*Tirpitz* Collection)

67. *Tirpitz* prepares for sea. The detail of the hinged bridge wing extension, necessary for conning a ship with such a wide beam in restricted conditions, is clear in this view, as are the radar antenna 'mattresses'. (*Tirpitz* Collection)

68. The bridge personnel take a soaking as the ship steams beam on to wind and sea. At bottom left can be seen inboard end of the opened bridge wing extension. (*Tirpitz* Collection)

69. The British were aware that *Tirpitz* was working-up in the Baltic, and the three major base ports of Kiel, Gdansk and Gotenhafen (Gdynia) were all regularly photographed by reconnaissance aircraft. In this view of Kiel, the camera has recorded not only *Tirpitz*, but also three Type VII U-boats (left), a 280-foot auxiliary alongside the wall, and two floating docks (upper right). (Imperial War Museum)

70. More rare was a photograph of *Tirpitz* at sea, the difficulty of locating her so far from the base of the reconnaissance aircraft and the likelihood of cloud in the area combining to reduce the chances of obtaining such a clear shot. (Imperial War Museum)

67

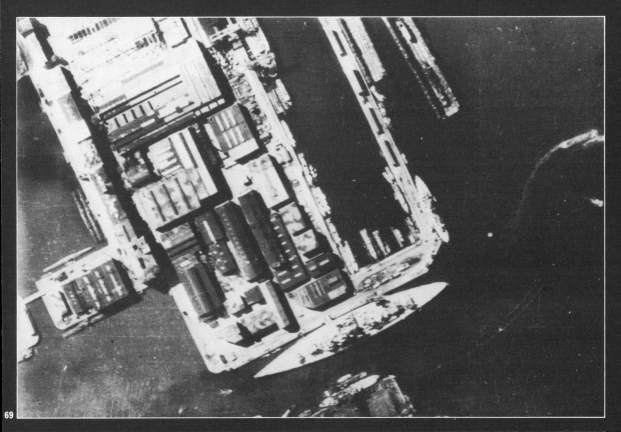

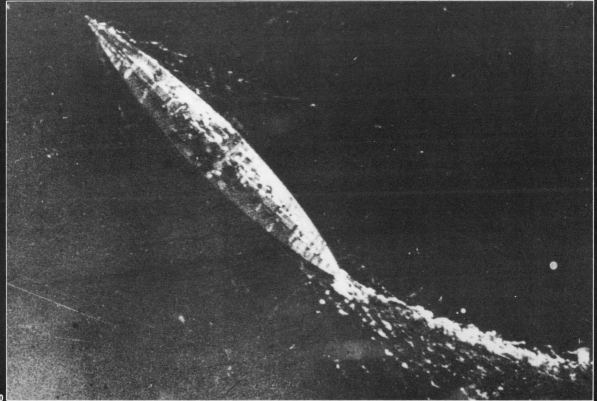

71

72

73

74

71, 72. *Tirpitz* was able to work-up in almost complete safety until 21 June 1941, free from surface or submarine attack, while danger from the air was insignificant. The ship could thus stop for seamanship exercises, such as launching and recovering the pulling cutter. The boat does not appear to be equipped with a patent disengaging gear, so that release from the falls depends upon co-ordination between the operators in the bow and stern to achieve simultaneous separation. (*Tirpitz* Collection)

73, 74. Streaming the minesweeping paravane, a combined 'kite' which supported a wire led out from the ship's stem to engage the cables of moored mines. The mines thus engaged would be unable to swing back against the ship's side and if their cables remained uncut they would be destroyed by the counter-mining charge attached to the paravane wire. (*Tirpitz* Collection)

75. Like most large ships, *Tirpitz* carried a few depth-charges, primarily for use as 'scare charges', and the release gear for these had also to be tested during the work-up. The boil of water caused by the explosion of the detonator is framed by the sturdy bracket of the ensign staff. (*Tirpitz* Collection)

76. Mechanical breakdowns had to be practised, in order to train the crew to react correctly to the consequences of battle damage as well as 'routine' failures. Steering a 45,000-ton battleship by hand was no job for lightweights. (*Tirpitz* Collection)

77. 'Stand-easy' — members of the forecastle party take a break. The Rheinmetall C30 20mm flak is well illustrated. (*Tirpitz* Collection)

77

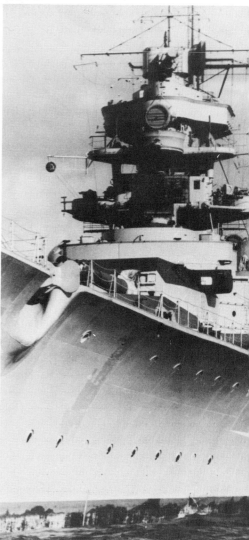

78

78. The 'sharp end' seen from the light flak platform below the main director tower, looking down to the director and radar 'mattress' on the roof of the oval conning-tower. (*Tirpitz* Collection)

79. The bridge structure of *Tirpitz*, showing the thickness of the main armour belt, and the various platforms around the central tower, including the signalling platforms and Admiral's Bridge (behind the lower director), the flak and searchlight platforms, and the air look-out position below the main director. (*Tirpitz* Collection)

80. The after superstructure, before the fitting of the stabilized flak director on the pedestal abaft the mainmast. (*Tirpitz* Collection)

81. A Type VII U-boat comes alongside *Tirpitz*. No contrast could be greater than that presented by these, the largest and the smallest of German ocean-going vessels, in terms of operational methods and results achieved. (*Tirpitz* Collection)

82. Continually busy aboard *Tirpitz* was her film team, making propaganda films, recording trials, and taking the still photographs which appear in this book. (*Tirpitz* Collection)

79 80

83, 84, 85, 86. The main armament trials, showing two-gun discharges from all four turrets. The muzzle blast effect on the water below 'Caesar' turret is obvious. The 1,764lb(800kg) L/4.4 armour-piercing shell from the 15in guns had an absolute maximum range of 26 statute miles (42km) and, striking at right angles, would penetrate 11.4 (289.6mm) inches of face-hardened armour at a range of 18.6 statute miles (32,800 yards/30km), the maximum practical range due to sighting considerations. (*Tirpitz* Collection)

84

86

87. The flash from the fore turrets highlights the port side of the superstructure while the blast creates a false 'bow wave' immediately below the expanding ball of propellant gas. (*Tirpitz* Collection)

88. A naval tug towed the canvas targets used for training the guns' crews and fire-control teams in firing on a moving target. (*Tirpitz* Collection)

89. Ratings from *Tirpitz* rigging the battle practice target alongside the tug. The target consisted of a series of floats, linked together to give the length required, and surmounted by a light framework which could be covered with canvas to varying heights to represent the freeboard of any ship up to the size of a battleship. (*Tirpitz* Collection)

90, 91. Two close misses short, are followed by a smoke display from the radio-controlled target ship indicating a direct hit. (*Tirpitz* Collection)

92. *Hessen*, a disarmed pre-dreadnought battleship, is examined for evidence of hits after a shoot by *Tirpitz*. The Control Vessel *Blitz*, a converted 1910-era torpedo-boat, lies alongside. (*Tirpitz* Collection)

93. Swabbing out the gun barrels after firing practice—a chore not to be undertaken on a wet and windy day in heavy seas. The thickness of the front face armour of the turrets is shown by the depth of the gun embrasures. (*Tripitz* Collection)

92

93

94, 95. Loading drill on a dummy 5.9in breech installed on the quarterdeck. The Krupps Seekanone C/28 was unusual in that it employed a sliding breech and a full length brass cartridge case, at a time when other navies were still using the interrupted screw breech and bagged powder charges for guns of greater than 5.5in calibre. With a well-trained crew, the opening rate of fire was as high as 8 rounds per minute, but the effort involved in hand loading and ramming a 95lb(43kg) projectile reduced this to a maximum of 5 rounds per minute after a short while. (*Tirpitz* Collection)

96. The dummy 4.1in flak breech, with the crew drilling under the eye of the Captain and Gunnery Officer. (*Tirpitz* Collection)

97. The real thing—a 4.1in mounting during a training shoot. (*Tirpitz* Collection)

98. Empty 4.1in round stowage cases are taken below after a shoot. The rail on the deck is part of the tracking which guides the aircraft from the hangar (in the background) on to the catapult track. (*Tirpitz* Collection)

94

97

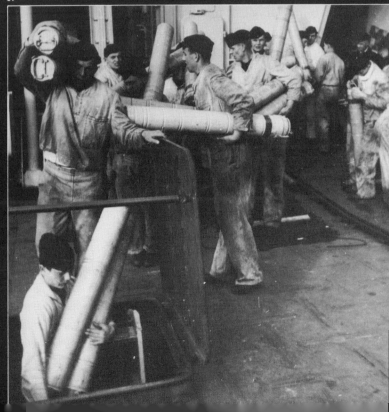

99. Practice for the light flak range-finding numbers, working in pairs with one man making the observations while the other takes notes. (*Tirpitz* Collection)

100. Range-finder at 'Action Stations': the first vierling ('quadruple') Rheinmetall 20mm flak C/38 mountings were installed during the late summer of 1941, providing a considerable increase in close-range automatic anti-aircraft firepower. (*Tirpitz* Collection)

101. A feature incorporated in *Tirpitz*, but not in *Bismarck*, was torpedo armament, a quadruple mount being fitted on each beam, just forward of the No 3 5.9in turret. Here, a dummy 21in 'fish' is launched from the starboard tubes. (*Tirpitz* Collection)

102. 'Caesar', 'Dora' and a quadruple 20mm flak mounting at the rear of the after director, line up for the camera towards the end of the work-up period. (*Tirpitz* Collection)

99

100

101

102

97

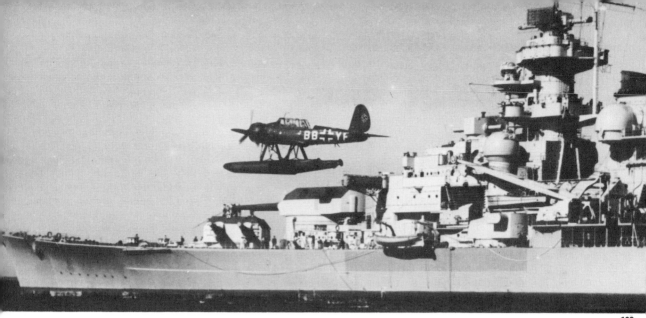

106

107

103-108. Aircraft also formed part of the ship's armament, providing over-the-horizon reconnaissance and fall-of-shot observation for the main armament. Up to six Arado Ar 196A floatplanes could be stowed, but the ship does not appear to have carried more than four at any one time. Designed for shipboard operation, with folding wings and catapult attachment points, the 970 hp BMW 122K-powered floatplane had a maximum speed of nearly 200mph, and the fuel tanks in the floats gave an endurance of more than four hours. Armament consisted of two flexible 7.92mm MG 17 machine-guns mounted in the Observer's cockpit, an MG 17 fixed in the starboard side of the engine cowling to fire through the airscrew arc, and two 20mm MG FF (Oerlikon) cannon in the wings. Outboard of the float struts, under each wing, was a bomb rack capable of carrying a 110lb(50kg) bomb.

This remarkable sequence of photographs shows the folded Ar 196 being fuelled in the starboard forward hangar, lashed down to its handling 'sledge' by canvas strops. The aircraft is then hauled out of the hangar by muscle-power and, still on its sledge, is rotated to line up with the catapult when its wings are spread for flight. The trolley which will provide the means of imparting the acceleration to the aircraft is then manoeuvred up behind the sledge and the extending arms take the weight of the aircraft while the sledge is removed to clear the track. The pneumatic/hydraulic catapult gave the 8,200lb Arado an 'end speed' of approximately 70mph. (*Tirpitz* Collection)

104

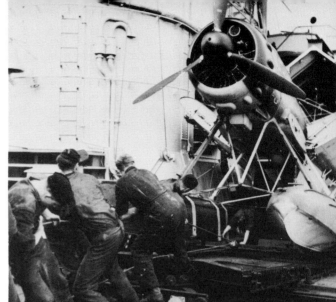

105

108

109

110

112

113

109-114. The Arado returns to the ship, crossing the stern as *Tirpitz* turns to starboard to create a smooth slick on which the aircraft can land in an otherwise choppy sea. After landing, the Observer climbs out of his cockpit and attaches a lifting becket to the arch of the pilot's windscreen and to two points on the engine cowling. As the aircraft comes under the crane, a special slip is made fast to the becket while lines from the ship steady the heavy pulley housing. Once attached and clear of the water, the aircraft's engine is switched off as it is swung inboard and repositioned on the catapult track, where the Luftwaffe pilot and Kriegsmarine Observer descend. (*Tirpitz* Collection)

115. Ancient and Modern: a pulling cutter comes up to one of the battleship's Arado Ar 196A-3 floatplanes to prepare to take it in tow. (*Tirpitz* Collection)

111

114

115

119

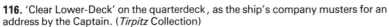

120

116. 'Clear Lower-Deck' on the quarterdeck, as the ship's company musters for an address by the Captain. (*Tirpitz* Collection)

117, 118. Leave: junior ratings line up to go aboard a harbour craft for a spell away from their 'tin monastery', while the Captain's motor boat leaves *Tirpitz* at a rather greater speed. (*Tirpitz* Collection)

119. Seen from the starboard quarter, *Tirpitz*'s huge beam and squat appearance heightens the menace expressed by the 15in guns of the after battery, elevated to the maximum 30°. (*Tirpitz* Collection)

120. An impressive propaganda photograph of the ship at high speed, with the director tower above the bridge turned to face the camera in order to conceal the radar 'mattress'. (*Tirpitz* Collection)

121. In mid-September 1941, *Tirpitz* made
ready for her first operation. Aerial
recognition flags were made up by painting
white disc, with a swastika skeleton, on
canvas. The flags were then laid out on the
forecastle and quarterdeck. (*Tirpitz*
Collection)

122. The German Baltic Fleet sailed for its
operational area off the Gulf of Finland on
26 September, to prevent the Russian Fleet
interfering with the German Army's advance
in Estonia and to guard against its possible
break-out to internment in Sweden. *Tirpitz*
seen leading the pocket-battleship *Admiral*

123 124

125

...eer and the light cruisers *Köln*, *Nürnberg*, ...zig and *Emden*, with two T1-class ...edo-boats in close company. (*Tirpitz* ...ection)

...Identification marks are painted on the ... of 'Caesar' turret as *Tirpitz* sails through ...misty Baltic, followed by *Scheer* and two ...he light cruisers. Russian submarines are ...rly not regarded as a threat, for the ships ...steaming at a modest speed in a regular ...mn—an ideal target for a submarine. ...*pitz* Collection)

...A 'Type 1935/37' torpedo-boat passes ...*itz* in foggy weather, the calm sea ...wing her to develop almost her full speed ...4 knots. (*Tirpitz* Collection)

...Off the Gulf of Finland, the Baltic Fleet ...ded into Northern and Southern Groups, ...former consisting of *Tirpitz*, *Nürnberg* and ...;, with a screen of destroyers and torpedo-...ts. (*Tirpitz* Collection)

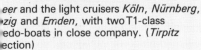

126. The Northern Group proceeded to an anchorage to the north of the Aland Islands where the ships were protected by the islands and Finnish minefields. Here, a 'Type 1934' Leberecht Maas-class destroyer passes *Tirpitz* in the anchorage while a Junkers Ju 88 patrols overhead. (*Tirpitz* Collection)

127. Also attached to the Northern Group was the 5th Minesweeping Flotilla of 'Type 1935' M-Boote, seen here secured alongside *Tirpitz*. (*Tirpitz* Collection)

128. An Arado is recovered, still carrying its 110lb(50kg) bombs, at the end of the 100th sortie from the ship. (*Tirpitz* Collection)

129. A Blohm und Voss Bv 138 flying boat, accompanied by one of the ship's Arados, flies past *Tirpitz* at the end of its anti-submarine patrol. (*Tirpitz* Collection)

128

129

132

133

130-133. On 12 January 1942, *Tirpitz* left Kiel and sailed through the Kaiser Wilhelm Kanal to return to Wilhelmshaven. (*Tirpitz* Collection)

134

138

135

136

137

134. 16 January 1942: *Tirpitz* arrives off Trondheim, which was to be her base for the next year. (*Tirpitz* Collection)

135. The battleship noses into her berth at the head of Foettenfjord, an arm of the main Trondheimfjord at some considerable distance from the town. (*Tirpitz* Collection)

136-140. The rigging of camouflage nets has already been practised during the months between the Åland Islands sortie and the departure for Norway, and with the aid of nature and a small forest of fir trees lashed to the guard rails and stuck in the anchor cable, *Tirpitz* soon looks like a battleship covered in snow and fir trees. The anti-torpedo boom seen in the reconnaissance photograph (No 120) is, in itself, a clear pointer to the presence of a major warship. (*Tirpitz* Collection and (120) Imperial War Museum)

144

141, 142. Arctic Sea smoke in Foettenfjord; mist caused by the air temperature falling below that of the sea. A light railway was built to connect the berth with the valley at the head of the fjord, for the purpose of supplying the ship. (*Tirpitz* Collection)

143. The guard and band turn out for a visit by Admiral Carls, C-in-C Gruppe Nord, his Chief of Staff and (centre) Admiral Schniewind, Flag-Officer, Battleships. (*Tirpitz* Collection)

144. The Russian steamer *Ijora*, straggling from convoy QP 8, sinks after being engaged by *Friedrich Ihn* on the afternoon of 7 March 1942. She was the only Allied ship to be seen by *Tirpitz*'s crew. (*Tirpitz* Collection)

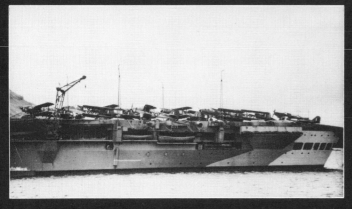

145. Ten Fairey Albacore torpedo-bombers of 817 and 832 Squadrons seen ranged on the after end of HMS *Victorious'* flight deck while the ship lies in Seidisfjord. Two Fulmar fighters of 809 Squadron are abaft the Albacores. (Imperial War Museum)

146. March 1942, 0917: 4A of 832 Squadron emerges from the cloud abeam of *Tirpitz* and begins to dive to an immediate attack. (Crown Copyright)

146

147. 0922: The turn to avoid the first·torpedo attack is observed by the aircraft of the first sub-flight of 817 Squadron and the second sub-flight of 832, which deliver a better co-ordinated attack some four minutes later. (Crown Copyright)

148. 0926: The view from one of the shadowing Albacores at the time of the last attack, with *Tirpitz* at the head of a 'question-mark' pattern track, in the centre of the picture. (Crown Copyright)

149. This photograph purports to show torpedo tracks close to *Tirpitz* during the attack on 9 March 1942, but in the author's opinion this is not the case: the wake does not correspond to the known track of the ship during the action, the main armament turrets are trained fore and aft (apparently with the muzzle covers still in place) and the AA director abaft the mainmast is also trained fore and aft. The streaks purporting to be torpedo tracks to starboard of *Tirpitz*'s stern appear to have been touched in to dramatize the incident. (*Tirpitz* Collection)

148

150, 151. *Tirpitz* under attack by the last two sub-flights, with splashes from 105mm, 37mm and 20mm projectiles hitting the water well short of the target, thus giving some credence to the Albacore aircrews' belief that the German sights were unable to cope with a target flying at the slow speed of 95-100 knots. (*Tirpitz* Collection)

150

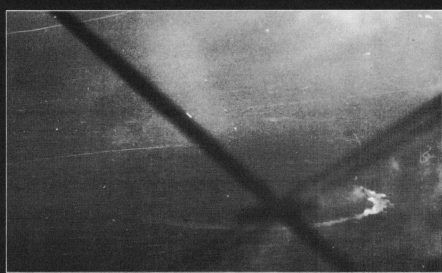

147

149

151

115

152, 153. Iron Crosses are awarded following the action on 9 March. The ceremony is likely to be protracted, to judge by the number of medals held by the Oberleutnant zur See. (*Tirpitz* Collection)

154-157. One of the modified Mark XIX mines, dropped by Halifaxes on the nights of 27/28 and 28/29 April 1942, is prepared for demolition and exploded close inshore. This was the weapon which the Germans believed was intended to be rolled under the ship, and which led to the laying of nets between the ship and the steeply sloping shore. (*Tirpitz* Collection)

158

159

158. A major event was the visit on 31 May 1942 of Grossadmiral Raeder, the C-in-C Navy, accompanied by Admiral Schniewind and Viceadmiral Oscar Kummetz, the new Flag-Officer, Cruisers (Oberbefehlshaber der Kreuzer), who is wearing the Knight's Cross over the Fleet service emblem (Flotten abzeichen). (*Tirpitz* Collection)

159. Admiral Raeder meets a selection of the ship's officers. Kapitän Topp's decorations include the Iron Cross of 1914, below the 1939 Bar, and the 'Cross of Honour of the World War' above the Fleet service emblem; below the Iron Cross is the oval Submarine service emblem (U-boats-Kriegsabzeichen) awarded to Topp for his service during the First World War. The Korvettenkapitän (second from the left) wears on his right breast the eight-pointed star of the Order of the German Cross (Kriegsorden des Deutschen Kreuzes), awarded only to holders of the Iron Cross 1st Class as recognition of further 'display of extraordinary gallantry in action', and the War Service of Merit Cross with swords (Kriegsverdienstkreuz mit Schwertern), awarded for special services while under fire. (*Tirpitz* Collection)

160-162. The ship's band gives performances: (160) marching through the quiet streets of Trondheim; (161) for the crew of the naval tanker *Nordmark*; and (162) for the crews of Leberecht *Maas*-Class destroyers which had accompanied *Tirpitz* on the March sortie. (*Tirpitz* Collection)

160

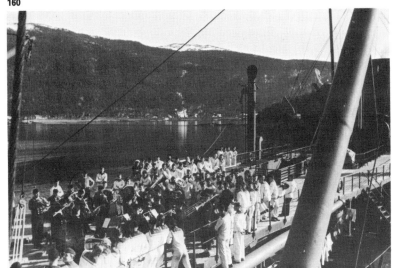

161

162

119

163. Convoy PQ 17 is sighted and photographed by a Luftflotte 5 shadower on 1 July. (*Tirpitz* Collection)

164. The pieces move out for the 'Knight's Move'—the heavy cruiser *Hipper* and three destroyers precede *Tirpitz* as the Trondheim Force heads for the open sea. (*Tirpitz* Collection)

163

164

165. *Karl Galster*, framed by the wing of an Ar 196 on *Tirpitz*'s catapult, with a backdrop of the Lofotens' rugged scenery, as the Force arrives at Gimsöstrommen. Shortly after this photograph was taken, *Hans Lody*, then *Galster* and *Theodor Riedel* struck rocks in a charted depth of over 20 fathoms (39m), leaving *Tirpitz* with an escort of only *Friedrich Ihn*, *Richard Beitzen* and two torpedo-boats which had escorted the tanker *Nordmark* to the Lofotens fuelling anchorage. (*Tirpitz* Collection)

166. *Friedrich Ihn* (*Z.14*) proceeded with *Tirpitz* and *Hipper* to Altenfjord to join the pocket-battleship force. Note that this older type of destroyer does not feature the raked bow and flared fo'c'sle which were intended to reduce the tendency to 'dig in' to heavy seas. Immediately ahead of the foremast she carries a 'Seetakt' radar antenna which must have been of indifferent use on bearings much abaft the beam. (*Tirpitz* Collection)

167. *Hipper*, *Scheer* and five of the seven destroyers follow *Tirpitz* down Altenfjord in the early afternoon of 5 July, bound for the interception of PQ 17. (*Tirpitz* Collection)

165

166

167

168. *Tirpitz* at anchor off Kaafjord in the late evening of 4 July—at the time that PQ 17's escort was receiving the fateful 'scatter' signal. Note the quadruple 20mm mounting on the starboard sponson on the funnel. (*Tirpitz* Collection)

169. An RAF Catalina flying boat at the Soviet base at Lake Grasnaya during the PQ 17 operation. In the background is a Beriev MBR-2 used by the VVS-VMF for coastal patrols. (Crown Copyright)

170. Admiral Schniewind and the Captain confer during the brief sortie. (*Tirpitz* Collection)

169

168

170

123

171

172

173

174

171. A Soviet Navy *K*-Class returns to Polyarno from a patrol off the Norwegian coast. Larger and faster than any other Allied submarine or German U-boat employed in the Arctic, they had been designed for ocean operations and, therefore, were not entirely suited to the primarily coastal campaign against German shipping and warships. (Novosti Press)

172. *Hipper* and *Scheer* rendezvous in Altenfjord with *Tirpitz* on 4 July 1942. (*Tirpitz* Collection)

173. A remarkable photograph of *Tirpitz* in Bogenfjord, near Narvik, taken by an agent on 8 August 1942. Nearer the head of the fjord is *Lützow*, painted in a similar two-tone grey "dazzle" camouflage scheme. (Crown Copyright)

174. Shore facilities for recreation were spartan at Foettenfjord, but included this open-air 'theatre' constructed by *Tirpitz*'s personnel in the spring of 1942. (*Tirpitz* Collection)

175. The officers fared rather better: Kapitän Topp poses in front of 'Perrig Heim', a chalet which served as a shore mess. (*Tirpitz* Collection)

176. The view from 'Perrig Heim' across Foettenfjord; the track leads down to the boat landing at the head of the fjord. (*Tirpitz* Collection)

175

176

177, 178. Victualling stores (including liquids) are transferred to *Tirpitz* from ships large and small. (*Tirpitz* Collection)

179, 180. RAF Coastal Command Photographic Reconnaissance Unit aircraft maintained a close watch on *Tirpitz* while she was being overhauled during December 1942 and January 1943. In these two low-level oblique views, taken on 12 December in Lofjord, the staging intended to carry camouflage netting can be seen around the battleship's bows and stern. (Imperial War Museum)

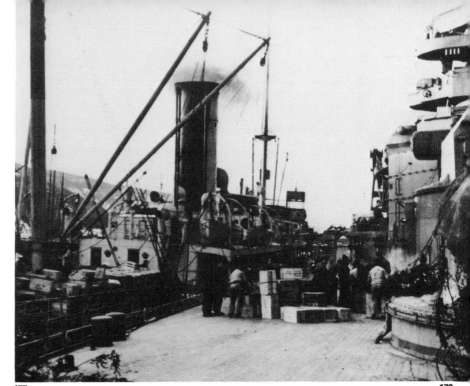

177

178

Glaube des Führers ist unser Glaube, Der Kampf des Führers — ist unser Kampf.

181

182

181. Christmas 1942—it is improbable that these cheerful matrosen were thinking similar thoughts to Hitler at this particular moment, whatever the writing on the bulkhead may imply. (*Tirpitz* Collection)

182. *Tirpitz* exercised in the Trondheim area from the end of January 1943. The work-up included seamanship drills, including replenishment of escorts at sea. Two 850-ton torpedo-boats, believed to be *T.7* and *T.15*, approach the 'tanker' as the latter's crew lays out hoses on the quarterdeck. (*Tirpitz* Collection)

183. The crew of a port-side 20mm quadruple mounting keep watch as the ship returns to Trondheimfjord. (*Tirpitz* Collection)

184. The aircraft's Observer manages to smile in spite of the cold: in the event of his aircraft coming to grief, he could not expect to remain conscious in the near-freezing sea for more than four minutes. Both the watch-keeping officers are wearing huge sheepskin coats which must have given the wearers greater protection from the elements than the Royal Navy's duffel coats. (*Tirpitz* Collection)

183

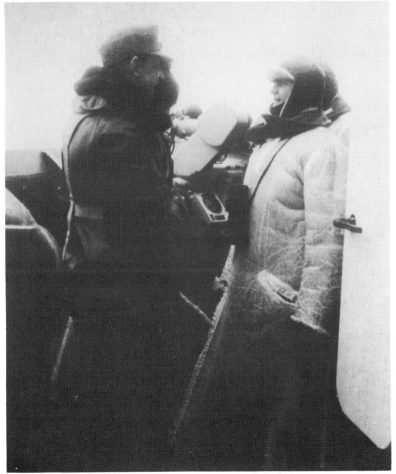

184

129

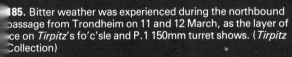

185. Bitter weather was experienced during the northbound passage from Trondheim on 11 and 12 March, as the layer of ice on *Tirpitz*'s fo'c'sle and P.1 150mm turret shows. (*Tirpitz* Collection)

186, 187. *Tirpitz* and her *Leberecht Maas*-Class destroyers pass up Westfjord and through the narrows to Bogenfjord on 3 March 1943. (*Tirpitz* Collection)

188, 189. Arrival in Altenfjord on 24 March. Members of the crew look at the scenery around the entrance to Kaafjord, *Tirpitz*'s base for the next 19 months. (*Tirpitz* Collection)

187

192

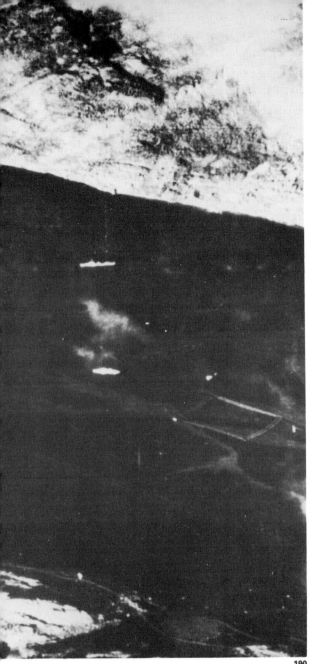

191

190. Although *Tirpitz*'s move to Kaafjord was followed by the Allies by means of wireless traffic interception, she was not sighted until 25 April (by a Soviet Naval Air Force aircraft) and the RAF did not obtain photographs until 10 May. This photograph, taken in late September 1943, after the X-craft attack, gives a useful panoramic view of the central section of Kaafjord, with its complicated net enclosures and steep sides. *Tirpitz* lies in deep shadow near the top left corner. (Imperial War Museum)

191. *Tirpitz* at sea on her last operation—the raid on Spitzbergen, where she arrived on the evening of 7 September 1943, flying the British White Ensign (a legitimate ruse de guerre, provided that it had been replaced by the German ensign before fire was opened). Note the covered 20mm Vierling mounting in the foreground: relatively small but highly effective, the mounting needed no external power sources and could thus be installed wherever a suitable position with good arcs of fire could be found. (*Tirpitz* Collection)

192. The ship's landing party returns with British and Norwegian prisoners. (*Tirpitz* Collection)

193. The floatplane returns from reconnaissance of Spitzbergen and misses the recovery strop at the first attempt—an unwelcome lapse as it obliged the Captain to remain at slow speed in potentially dangerous waters. (*Tirpitz* Collection)

190

193

194. HMS *Bonaventure*, a Clan Line freighter requisitioned and purchased while building, and completed as a depot ship for midget submarines. Cradles were provided for X-craft in the forward and after well decks, the midgets being handled by the heavy-lift derricks (stowed vertically against the kingposts). (Crown Copyright)

195. An X-craft on the surface, the commanding officer holding on to the partially-raised pivotting periscope tube — the only available support on the flush, narrow casing. (Crown Copyright)

196. A composite photograph of *Tirpitz* lying in the Barbrudalen enclosure on 22 September 1943. Part of a collection taken to illustrate the German 'post mortem' report, it is of very poor quality but gives a fair idea of the battleship's light grey and black 'dazzle' camouflage scheme. (*Tirpitz* Collection)

197. A Verposten-boot at the entrance to the Barbrudalen net through which Lieutenant Cameron's *X-6* penetrated. (*Tirpitz* Collection)

198. The spot and the circle beside the numeral '2' indicate, respectively, the positions at which *X-7* (Lieutenant Place) was seen to sink, and where Sub-Lieutenant Aitken surfaced after escaping, three hours later. Note that *Tirpitz*'s main topmast has been brought down by the whip of the ship in the explosions. (*Tirpitz* Collection)

194

196

197

195

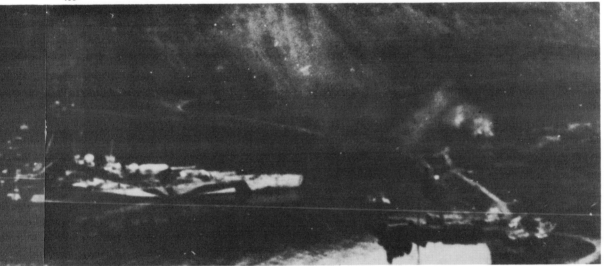

198

199

200

199, 200. German salvage teams salvaged *X-7*, less the bow section, and beached the midget on the Barbrudalen shore for close examination on 4 October 1943. Following the survey, some instruments and fittings were removed for delivery to Germany and the hull was towed out into the fjord and scuttled. (*Tirpitz* Collection)

201. *Tirpitz* lying in the Barbrudalen enclosure in which she was attacked by the X-Craft on 22 September 1943. This high-definition reconnaissance photograph was taken by a Spitfire flying from a Russian airfield.

201

202. Commander (Operations) briefs the aircrew of No 8 Torpedo-Bomber-Reconnaissance Wing with the aid of a scale model on the worn carpet of HMS *Furious'* Wardroom ante-room. (Imperial War Museum)

203. A Barracuda in flight carrying the 1,600lb American-supplied armour-piercing bomb. (Crown Copyright)

204. Explosive graffiti: the suspension lug of the 1,600lb bomb is amidships, and the torpedo 'sway braces' hold the bomb's nose and tail to prevent lateral movement. No ejection yoke was available, so the Barracuda was limited to a maximum practical dive-angle of about 60° and thus was classed as a 'glide-bomber', rather than a true dive-bomber. (Imperial War Museum)

205. The Hellcats of 804 Squadron from up astern of HMS *Emperor* as 800 Squadron's aircraft are brought up from the hangar to prepare for the second wave of the strike on 3 April 1944. (Imperial War Museum)

202

203

204

205

139

206. The Barracudas of the first wave pass to the west of Langfjord, where a tanker and two destroyers lie at anchor. Flying at about 3,000 feet to clear the mountain peaks, the Barracudas have still 15 miles to run to Kaafjord. (Crown Copyright)

207. The smokescreen begins to spread and *Tirpitz* opens fire as the first fighters begin their flak-suppression attack from the north-west. (Imperial War Museum)

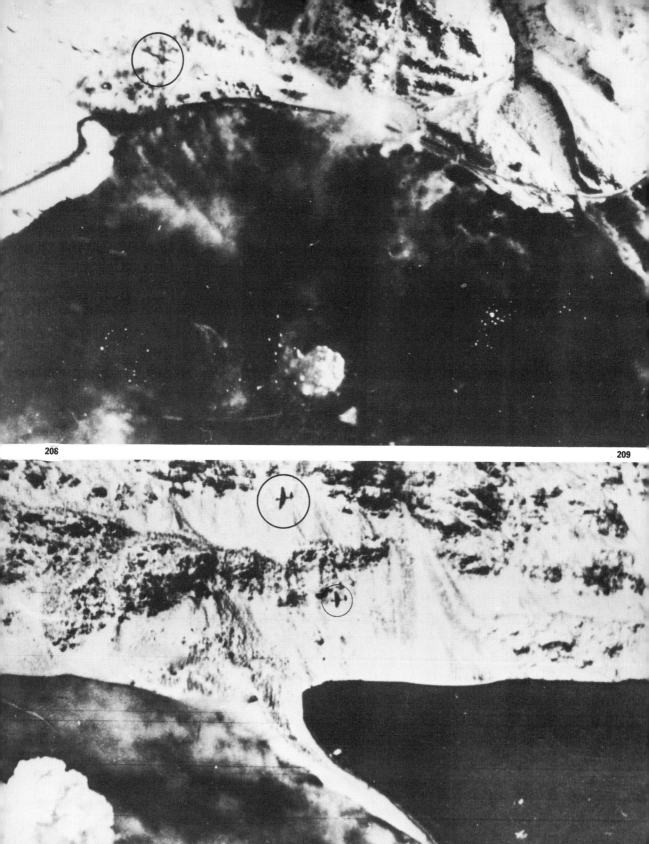

208. A thick 'ball' of smoke arises from the explosion of one of the bombs which struck forward as a section of Barracudas attacks from the south. Note diving Barracuda (circled). (Crown Copyright)

209. Taken shortly after the preceding shot, this photograph includes sufficient of the ship to show that she is already heavily on fire in the area of the bridge and funnel. Two Barracudas can be seen banking steeply after recovering from their dives. (Imperial War Museum)

210. A No 52 TBR Wing Barracuda seen (top of picture) immediately before releasing its three 500lb bombs. The smoke screen is obviously ineffective and the column of steam from the jammed siren can be seen rising from *Tirpitz*'s starboard side amidships. (Imperial War Museum)

210

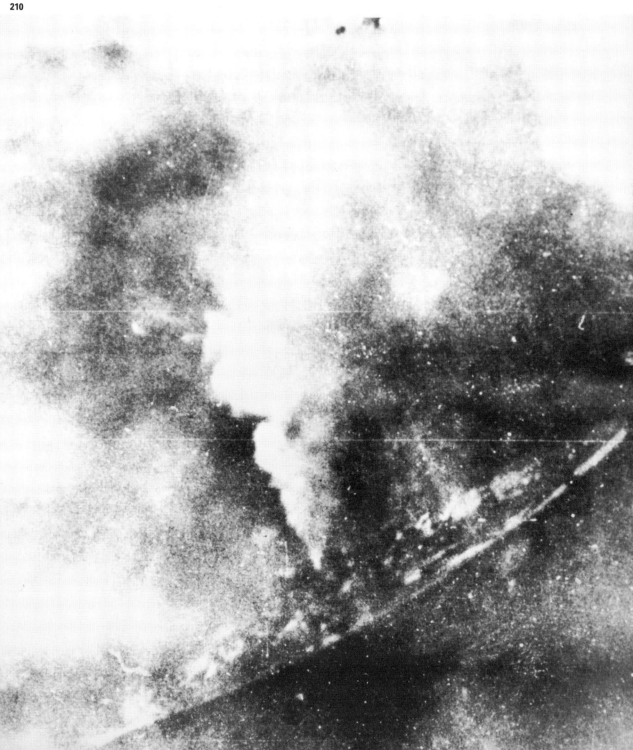

211. The Carrier Force awaits the return of the strikes at about 0700 on 3 April; seen from *Emperor*, HMS *Searcher*, *Furious* and *Pursuer*, with the battleship *Anson* in the background. (Imperial War Museum)

212. The Barracuda with a hung-up 1,600lb bomb lands back aboard *Furious* while two other aircraft from the first strike run into the 'slot' to join the landing circuit. HMS *Belfast* is on the carrier's starboard quarter. (Imperial War Museum)

213. 898 Squadron FM-1 Wildcats return to *Searcher*. (via D. J. Frearson)

214. *Tirpitz* was repaired in a new enclosure adjacent to the spit of land across the fijord from the berth which she had occupied since March 1943. Here she was photographed by a PRU Mosquito on the evening of 12 July 1944, lying with six lighters and small craft, four boats and a repair stage alongside. The starboard seaplane crane has been removed and the deck has been camouflaged to give a mottled effect. (Imperial War Museum)

215

216

215. Barracuda 'M' of 830 Squadron is airborne before reaching the wooden ramp built over *Furious'* forward round-down (to extend the flight deck length available for take-off), in spite of the weight of the 1,600lb bomb. By this time (17 July 1944), nearly all the aircraft serving in the front-line Barracuda squadrons had been modified to carry the big bomb. (Imperial War Museum)

216. *Furious* (foreground), *Formidable* and *Anson* and a destroyer within sight of the North Cape during the July strike operation 'Mascot'. (Crown Copyright)

217. One of *Tirpitz*'s 20mm multiple mountings in action. The lack of any form of splinter shield on or around the mounting rendered the guns' crews liable to serious casualties, which were duly sustained whenever Royal Navy fighters attacked. (*Tirpitz* Collection)

217

218. Fairey Fireflies received their baptism of fire on 10 August 1944, when they supported a minelaying operation in the Leads, south of *Tirpitz*'s anchorage. A division of *Indefatigable*'s 1770 Squadron is here seen escorting the inbound minelaying Avengers. (Crown Copyright)

219. Operation 'Goodwood': *Formidable*'s Corsairs and Barracudas are 'spotted' on deck prior to arming. (Imperial War Museum)

220. 22 August 1944: Corsairs of 1841 Squadron take departure for the first strike with HMS *Devonshire* and HMS

Trumpeter (behind) in the background. (Imperial War Museum)

221. On the afternoon of 22 August 1944, the Hellcat fighter-bombers and Firefly flak-suppression aircraft caught *Tirpitz* before the smokescreen was complete. This photograph was taken after the attack, and *Tirpitz*'s hull can be distinguished in the top right-hand quadrant. (Crown Copyright)

222. 24 August: the Force turns into wind to launch the third strike of Operation 'Goodwood'. Left to right: *Formidable*, *Devonshire*, *Indefatigable* and *Duke of York*. (Crown Copyright)

221

222

223. 'Goofers' view of *Formidable*'s range of Corsairs and Barracudas during the launch on 29 August. The two bomb-armed Corsairs can be seen on the port deck edge, the 1,000lb bomb being slung on a pylon below the starboard wing-root. (Crown Copyright)

224, 225. *Indefatigable*'s Barracudas seen approaching the coast at low level to avoid detection by German radar and then climbing as they pass Silden Island, 35 miles north-west of Kaafjord. (A. J. Ward)

223

224

226. The 'ten-tenths' smokescreen which greeted the last 'Goodwood' strike, on 29 August, reached up to nearly 2,000 feet and totally obscured the target. (Crown Copyright)

227. The Seafire FIIIs of *Indefatigable*'s No 24 Fighter Wing were used for defensive patrols and on diversionary strafing attacks during 'Goodwood'. Here, an 887 Squadron aircraft floats over the arrester wires but might, with luck, catch the lowered No 3 Barrier and thus avoid a headlong arrival in the raised No 2 Barrier. (Fleet Air Arm Museum)

228. A Blohm und Voss Bv 138C long-range maritime patrol flying boat is unmoored at Banak, the scene of the destruction of four of these valuable aircraft by 887 Squadron on the morning of 22 August; two more were shot down near the Fleet by 894 Squadron Seafires in the afternoon of the same day. (*Tirpitz* Collection)

154

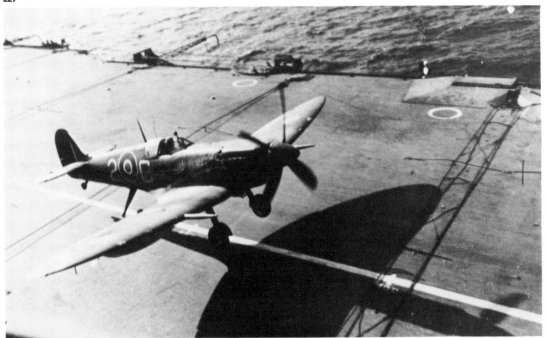

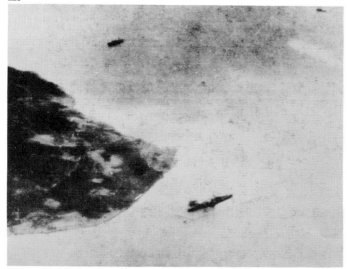

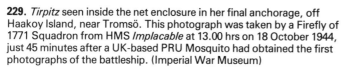

229. *Tirpitz* seen inside the net enclosure in her final anchorage, off Haakoy Island, near Tromsö. This photograph was taken by a Firefly of 1771 Squadron from HMS *Implacable* at 13.00 hrs on 18 October 1944, just 45 minutes after a UK-based PRU Mosquito had obtained the first photographs of the battleship. (Imperial War Museum)

230. The last attack on *Tirpitz* by the Lancasters of Nos 9 and 617 Squadrons, RAF, as depicted in 'The sinking of the *Tirpitz*' by Gerald Coulson, GAvA. This painting is the property of the Ministry of Defence, and is hanging at the RAF College, Cranwell.

231. *Tirpitz*'s bows can just be seen protruding from the lower left-hand edge of the welter of smoke and steam caused by the direct hits with 12,000lb bombs; note the detonation of the 'Tallboy' on the shore of Haakoy Island. (Imperial War Museum)

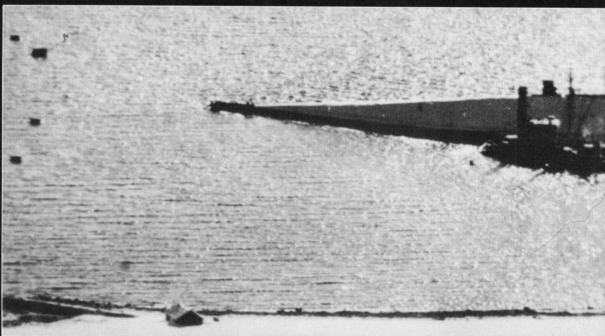

233

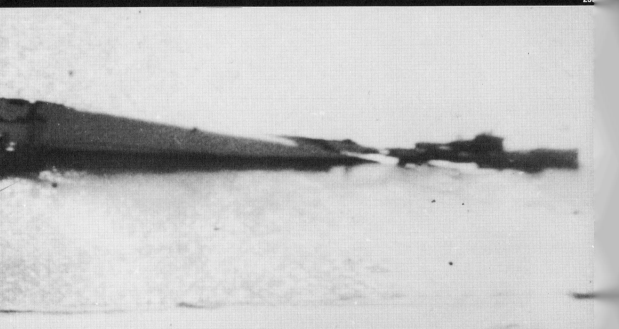

232, 233. Finis! These remarkable photographs were the last to be taken of *Tirpitz* during the war. On 23 March 1945, a Mosquito of No 540 Squadron, RAF Coastal Command, made what was referred to as a 'post mortem sortie' and instead of remaining at height for the usual vertical views, descended to a very low level to take clear photographs of the capsized and snow-covered hull of Germany's last dreadnought battleship. (Imperial War Museum)

234, 235. Immediately after the end of the War in Europe, a Bomber Command damage assessment survey team was despatched to Tromsö to examine the hulk of *Tirpitz*. German salvage ships had removed the propellers and the main armoured belt on the starboard side, and holes had been cut in the exposed side and bottom in the search for bodies and recoverable equipment. Note that the starboard deck edge is just exposed at this stage of the tide. (Crown Copyright)

236. A German prisoner of war standing on the side of *Tirpitz*'s upturned hull gives a sense of scale to the 12.6in armour of the main belt. The 5in upper belt is below his feet, and above his head is one of the holes cut in an attempt to rescue members of the crew trapped during the final attack (Crown Copyright)